# Better
# BOOK
# Clubs

"Children need and deserve time to be in community with one another to talk about books in ways that grows their comprehension and increases their love of reading. And teachers need and deserve this excellent book by Sara Kugler for the tips, tools, and strategies to help us lead these book clubs well."

**JENNIFER SERRAVALLO**
author of *The Writing Strategies Book*
and *The Reading Strategies Book*

"I dare you to read just the first three pages of *Better Book Clubs* and not fall in love with it. In the very first sentence, Sara Kugler introduces us to the idea of book clubs as 'a practice of liberation' and a path to growing powerful readers both inside and outside the classroom. And with every subsequent turn of the page, Sara draws us a roadmap to a book club practice that is both accessible and aspirational. This book is full of the kinds of tips, lessons, and tools that will help teachers move from big ideas to action, and I can't wait to see the tremendous impact it will make in classrooms!"

**KASSIA OMOHUNDRO WEDEKIND**
coauthor of *Hands Down, Speak Out,*
and author of *Math Exchanges*

"The introduction of *Better Book Clubs* makes the case that book clubs are for all kids. If you still need some convincing, flip to the last chapter and listen to the growth Sara Kugler's students made from February to May. These are the conversations our kids deserve, and these are the opportunities we dream of facilitating as teachers. No need to wait. Sara knew we needed this book, so she decided to sit down next to us and coach us along the way."

**KATHLEEN FAY**
author of *Powerful Book Introductions*
and *Becoming One Community*

"In *Better Book Clubs*, Sara has made the aspirational (I'd love to do book clubs) practical (I can do book clubs). Research, classroom stories, and practical strategies blend with Sara's passion to make not only a helpful professional text but an enjoyable one. A must-read for anyone interested in facilitating rich dynamic thinking and talking around books."

**KRISTI MRAZ**
coauthor of *Kids First from Day One*
and *Mindset for Learning*

"We all know the autonomy, engagement, and relationships built during book clubs are critical for students. We also know how difficult teaching these days can be and how much needs to get done right now. There are valid reasons to view book clubs as something extra that can be put off until we accomplish the important things. In her book, Sara makes a compelling case for why and how book clubs are important. She not only explains what fundamental literacy skills and habits are developed through book clubs, but also takes us step-by-step through ways to help make them happen well. Warm, practical, and very realistic, this is a great book for both veteran and novice book club teachers."

**M. COLLEEN CRUZ**
author of *Risk. Fail. Rise.: A Teacher's Guide to Learning from Mistakes* and the *Writers Read Better* Series

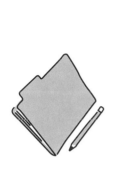

# Better BOOK Clubs

## Deepening Comprehension and Elevating Conversation

**SARA KUGLER**

www.stenhouse.com
Portsmouth, New Hampshire

www.stenhouse.com

Library of Congress Cataloging-in-Publication Data

Names: Kugler, Sara, author.
Title: Better book clubs : deepening comprehension and elevating
  conversation / Sara Kugler.
Description: Portsmouth, New Hampshire : Stenhouse Publishers, [2022] |
  Includes bibliographical references and index. |
Identifiers: LCCN 2021055453 (print) | LCCN 2021055454 (ebook) | ISBN
  9781625313928 (paperback) | ISBN 9781625313935 (ebook)
Subjects: LCSH: Book clubs (Discussion groups) | Reading
  comprehension—Study and teaching (Elementary) | Reading (Elementary) |
  Children—Books and reading.
Classification: LCC LC6631 .K84 2022  (print) | LCC LC6631  (ebook) | DDC
  372.41/62—dc23/eng/20220601
LC record available at https://lccn.loc.gov/2021055453
LC ebook record available at https://lccn.loc.gov/2021055454

Cover and interior design by Jill Shaffer
Typesetting by Eclipse Publishing Services

Printed in the United States of America
This book is printed on paper certified by third-party standards for sustainably managed forestry.

28  27  26  25  24  23  22    4371    9  8  7  6  5  4  3  2  1

**To Mom,**
my first and best writing teacher.

**To Dad,**
who taught me to see pure genius in every single child.

**To Alex,**
who believed in pizza night and this book.

I SUBMIT that what the teacher is giving up is control but not power . . . the measure of her loss of control may be precisely the measure of her gain in power, for if her goal in such events is to better understand the children's thinking, then the more that the thinking can reveal itself, the more fully she reaches her goal.

—Judith Lindfors

# Contents

# Acknowledgments

I DON'T KNOW HOW I got this lucky. Each move in my career landed me next to some of the most brilliant, innovative, and dedicated educators. I began my career working with Amy Greene, and I owe my indelible sense of workshop teaching to your mentorship during my very first year in the classroom.

In Brooklyn, I somehow managed to study under Colleen Cruz, who taught me what true student independence and agency look like in a classroom. I hope you're right about most things, because I quote you often. At the Teachers College Reading and Writing Project, few people shaped my ideas about Book Clubs more than Brooke Geller, Cory Gillette, Jen Serravallo, and Lucy Calkins, who also taught me how to study students closely in order to see their strengths.

In Fairfax County, I almost lost track of the people I learned from and was inspired by. It's an embarrassment of riches over here. Stacey Duff and the staff of Mason Crest Elementary helped shape this book through their collaboration, inquiry, and student-centered approach. Thank you to Cait Fiocchi, Grace Choi, Raven Compton, Mary Kate DeRose, Lauren Austin, Daisy Bokus, Jean Sowers, Rachel Gottheim, Ashley Tingler, and Kassia Wedekind, who have been my thought partners and my most trusted sources of feedback on all things teaching. Amanda Dey, Aly McCarty, and Evelyn Wells—thank you for your adventurous teaching spirit and for your belief that this is the right work for all kids. To all the Summer Literacy Symposium presenters—our work together inspired the ideas in this book. Kath Fay and Suzanne Whaley, you have pushed my thinking at every turn and helped me outgrow myself each year.

A special thank you to my editor, Terry Thompson. I know everyone says this, but you really are incomparable. Thanks for having patience and kindness and so much skill. And thank you to Mark Corsey and Shannon St. Peter for helping this book take shape.

After each day of working with the absolute best, I get to return home to Maxine and Elias for inspiration. I get to witness their love of reading and writing and their dedication to talking about it *all*. I work to make this place better for you.

# The Purpose and Power of Book Clubs

Participating in book clubs is, and has always been, a practice of liberation.

In basements and backrooms, revolutionaries gather to discuss political ideas found in manifestos. At universities, students sit around tables or pull chairs into a circle to examine texts that have been deemed canonical and texts that challenge the very concept of a literary canon. In yeshivas, rabbinical students gather around the Talmud to discuss the various interpretations of Jewish law. In homes, neighbors gather around a coffee table with teacups or wine glasses to discuss a novel that opened their eyes to new worlds.

This is what book clubs do in the real world. This is what book clubs can and should do in schools. Instead of just preparing students for (more) school, experiences in school should prepare students for a life—and, I would argue, a rich, literate life.

Beyond their academic potential, book clubs teach us about being a part of a community. They teach us how to listen deeply in order to connect with each other. They teach us to stretch beyond our own experiences and understandings of the word and the world.

As I write this, we are over a year into the global pandemic. While many of us are starting to tiptoe back into our workplaces and schools, we're taking stock of what was lost and what was gained this year. Parents mourned the loss of chorus concerts where second graders show how to sing in rounds while hammering the xylophone. The energy and hum of an office or a classroom was mostly missed. Despite all of this, book clubs were one of the things that survived and even thrived this year. We could still pick a title, reserve it from our local libraries or get it on our tablets. We could still sit together (around an outdoor fire pit or on Zoom) and talk about the language we loved, the ideas we developed, and our critiques of the book. Oprah relaunched her book club. Instagram influencers started new clubs with the hashtag #bookstagram. This kind of emotional and intellectual connection turned out to be something we all needed as we spent most of our time at home.

It wasn't just adults who needed book clubs. More than half of the children in the U.S. spent almost a full year engaging in schooling through a computer screen. They missed the constant face-to-face interactions, and it's no secret that virtual school created roadblocks to authentic and frequent talk among peers. In this less-familiar territory, some of us fell back into some of our old patterns of over-facilitating and controlling conversations between kids. But book clubs offered me and my students a way back into authentic and meaningful conversations about texts.

A month into the pandemic, I finally got one of my fourth-grade book clubs back together on Google Meet. Not surprisingly, the students were desperate for an excuse to meet and talk with each other. This book club, whose members called themselves The Unsinkables after their obsession with books about the *Titanic*, was so desperate for social interaction that when school ended in June, one member asked, "Can we just keep meeting once a week during the summer?" And we did. We read articles about the ocean, digital books about the Lamborghini Aventador, and historical fiction novels from their favorite series. Our time together provided intellectual stimulation, a chance to be seen by peers and an adult, and an emotional connection that none of us were getting enough of this year.

To participate in book clubs, The Unsinkables didn't need a set of rules or assigned roles or to be "held accountable" for their talk. They needed purpose—a reason to meet with each other that didn't come from an assignment. They needed a sense of responsibility—not to an outsider but to each other. And they needed engaging texts they had chosen themselves.

That's what book clubs in the real world need. And the closer we can get to creating classrooms that prepare kids for the world outside of school, the better off our kids will be when they leave school for good. Our job isn't to control students until they're free. Our job is to help students get free.

## Authentic Book Club Experiences

In her book *Study Driven* (2006), Katie Wood Ray advises us teachers to begin each unit of study in writing by immersing ourselves and our students in the kinds of writing we are trying to create. We should collect writing from the world, read and reread those texts with highlighters and sticky notes in hand, and notice how they're written. We should try to name the things real writers do to craft effective pieces so that our students can try those techniques in their own writing. By grounding ourselves in authentic writing first, we can ensure that we are teaching, and students are learning, tools and techniques that will be useful to them when they are writing for purposes beyond school. With this practice, Katie Wood Ray is reminding us to start with what is authentic. What do real writers do?

I would suggest we utilize this same question in reading. What do real readers do? What are the ways they talk about texts and use those conversations to understand themselves, explore words beyond their own, take action, and make their world better? We aren't here merely to play school, to reenact the ways in which we were taught as students, facing the front of the room, standing in silent lines, sitting in seats, listening to a teacher. This isn't the school experience any of us imagine for our students. Instead, we strive to create a place where they can learn how to be citizens. Citizens participate fully, citizens speak truth to power, citizens see injustice and call it by name. Authentic book club interactions are a step in this direction.

Surprisingly, even as we want these things for our learning communities, we sometimes get in our own way when, in an attempt to ensure learning is taking place, we guide our students' responses toward a particular outcome. Whatever our motives, this safety blanket of sorts, this need to have everything fall just right, can keep us from developing authentic book club experiences. I understand on a very personal level the feeling of needing to control things. My husband jokes that he can tell when I'm stressed because I tidy up at home, putting all the mail in neat piles, pushing in the dining room chairs, and obsessively vacuuming the kitchen floor. When I can't control the important stuff, I control the piles and dust. Controlling something brings a sense of calm. As mandated tests become more frequent and the stakes become higher, the adults in our buildings, the ones who have power, might feel the need to exert control over *something*. Usually what we exert control over is children. We separate desks so kids can talk less and listen to us more; we straighten the rows of students so they face the teacher. We tidy up.

Make no mistake—I know how important structures and routines can be, and you'll find lots of ideas and tips for these throughout this book. However, if the end goals are structures, routines, and directions, book clubs become just another way we play school without thinking deeply and critically about which practices actually ready students for authentic, meaningful experiences with reading. Instead, structures and routines should offer supports for independent thinking and pathways for self-directed learning.

In writing a professional book about book clubs, I know I run the risk of promoting a practice that becomes another procedure for teachers to teach and for students to follow. That is not my hope or intent. I do not want reproducibles, worksheets, and adorably themed handouts to become stand-ins for the real, brave teaching that kids need. My intent is to provide students with the most empowering, authentic reading experience I can possibly provide—access to books they want to read, instruction that leads them to develop ideas and responses to those books, opportunities to talk to their peers about their thinking, and feedback that recognizes growth. This in itself is a type of freedom—and one that is often not granted to all students in all schools.

## The Benefits of Book Clubs

If you've ever participated in a book club, as a child or as an adult, you've experienced its benefits firsthand. Through your discussion with others, you've probably deepened your understanding of the texts you read, seeing things in the writing you missed on your own. You've probably considered others' interpretations and ideas that didn't even cross your mind when you read the book the first time. Building a shared and complex under-standing of a book is part and parcel of the reading work inherent in book clubs. However, it's worth considering other important benefits that come from participating in a book club—emotional connection with others, a heightened sense of engagement in reading, and an increase in motivation to read more and read widely.

In addition to all these important benefits, the practice of talking with others about the books we read also helps improve our comprehension. The more we know about the reading process, the more we understand the critical role oral language development plays in reading comprehen-sion. Students develop oral language from a very young age and can under-stand language much earlier than they can produce it. Children develop oral language by listening to others communicate and by participating in conversations themselves.

Developing more sophisticated oral language serves children well as they read increasingly demanding texts that include literary language, content-specific vocabulary, and complex sentence structure. As students read the words on the page, they must also hear them in their own head. The process by which readers internalize written words as oral language is called "listening comprehension."

Readers need to listen to themselves read, and if the written words they encounter are already familiar to them from an oral-language con-text, they're more likely to understand what they're reading. Therefore, developing students' oral language leads to increased listening compre-hension. And strong listening comprehension is a key to successful reading comprehension (Burkins and Yates 2021). In book clubs, as students par-ticipate in academic discourse about text, they're developing sophisticated oral language, which fortifies their listening comprehension and increases their reading comprehension (see Figure 0.1).

Figure 0.1

Book clubs are just one way, one opportunity throughout your day, to teach students how to have academic conversations. All students are learning English, but if the students in your classroom or school are learn-ing English in addition to other languages spoken in their homes, it is even more essential to guarantee time each day to engage in meaningful conversations.

The benefits of book clubs aren't limited to the pages of a book. Book clubs also provide a sense of community and belonging for students. While other small-group experiences are led by teachers, book clubs can serve as a time during which students feel more ownership and agency. Even clubs that start out needing heavy teacher support can be taught to function with increasing independence. Time spent engaging in a dialogue about a shared text provides students with the same sense of pleasure and connection it provides adults. There's no reason students need to leave school before they engage in a book club.

As you can imagine, book clubs have the potential to increase students' engagement and widen their exposure to a variety of texts. Introducing book clubs reenergizes students by increasing their social interactions within an academic context. A fourth-grade teacher once told me that her students begged for more reading time once she launched books clubs. They wanted more time for independent reading so that they would have more to discuss with their clubs. I too have seen how book clubs can transform students. I remember a sixth-grade boy who initially claimed to hate poetry. After reading *Long Way Down*, a novel in verse by Jason Reynolds, with his book club, he ended up leading deep conversations with his friends and sharing ideas about his favorite lines and scenes.

While bureaucracies measure one kind of reading progress, teachers know that these levels of engagement, motivation, positive identity, and relationships with peers, combined with a general sense of belonging, are also keys to success.

## How This Book Works

This book is designed for classroom teachers, literacy coaches, and anyone interested in developing authentic academic discourse among their students. Though we'll keep our lens focused on books clubs, the information you'll find here could be just as easily applied to math clubs (talking about data), science clubs (talking about research), history clubs (talking about historical events and primary source documents), movie clubs, cooking clubs, art clubs. The possibilities are endless.

I'm a person who is obsessed with process. I love thinking not just about *what* I'm trying to accomplish but about *how* I'm going to accomplish it. Which processes have I used before that have worked? Which will I use this time? This book focuses both on *what* to assess and teach and also on *how* to assess and teach—in other words, it presents assessment and instructional processes that help students understand texts and talk about them with growing independence.

*Better Book Clubs* is divided into six cumulative chapters that will help you get clubs up and running with your readers. Chapter 1 describes the conditions and routines you'll need in order to launch book clubs. Chapter 2 explores methods of instruction that serve as temporary scaffolds for students as you teach them to become more independent. Chapter 3 provides logistics and options for launching book clubs and building students' independence as they transition from teacher-led to student-led book clubs.

In Chapter 4, we take a deep dive into formative assessment. I share tools, lenses, and methods to assess the current sophistication of the readers in your class. I also demonstrate how to use the data you collect to identify students' strengths, as well as next steps they're ready to tackle. Chapter 5 examines the decisions we make before we teach and also those we make in the moment to best support readers as they grow. And lastly, Chapter 6 rounds things out with an analysis of observations—both the daily, small shifts and the long game of major growth toward sophisticated conversation and, in turn, deeper comprehension.

In the pages of this book, you'll find inspiration and ideas to get you started, whether you're new to book clubs, you're developing your confidence around them, or you're ready to refine your responsiveness within a familiar practice. This book is designed to give you practical tools and strategies that allow you and the students in your classroom to experience growth. But most importantly, it's my deepest belief that your students will find joy and meaning and connection by talking about books and sharing their own ideas. And it is my greatest hope that the book clubs you guide will leave students feeling the way Anne Lamott (1994) does about books:

> What a miracle it is that out of these small, flat, rigid squares of paper unfolds world after world after world, worlds that sing to you, comfort and quiet or excite you. Books help us understand who we are and how we are to behave. They show us what community and friendship mean; they show us how to live and die.

# CHAPTER 1

# Grounding Book Clubs in the Predictability of Workshop

**D**URING MY FIRST YEAR of teaching, I worked closely with an ESOL teacher, Phyllis Williams, who would support my class during reading workshop. As I struggled to teach routines and procedures while maintaining some semblance of control that first week, Phyllis smiled at me patiently and said, "Structure liberates, doesn't it?" I'm sure I nodded knowingly but had little idea of what in the world she could mean by this. It was only weeks later that I started to see the effects that teaching consistent routines had on my energetic bunch of second graders. Over time, students found their spots on the rug with more ease, they (mostly) stopped elbowing each other to get to their book boxes, and they settled into a productive buzz of independent reading more quickly. Three weeks into school, our routines were humming along like well-oiled machines, and we could shift our focus to more academic endeavors.

Phyllis's words came to life as I realized that when our time with students includes consistent routines, expectations, and materials, students can focus on new learning. If the tasks and patterns of each day change, their mental stamina (not to mention time) is taken up by figuring out where to go, what to do, and how much time they have. When routines are consistent day in and day out, children can concentrate on other things—namely, what we want to teach them about being readers.

I'm a big believer that anything we do in the classroom has to have legs outside of the context of school. Real readers find ways to think and talk with other people about the texts they're reading, so teaching students to participate in book clubs is an essential part of their literacy journey. Placing book clubs in a structure such as reading workshop provides the predictability that gradually builds independence. In this chapter, I'll review what is probably most familiar to you—the structure and purpose of each component found in a traditional reading workshop. As I go, I'll share how each component might look and feel slightly different once you introduce book clubs into your workshop.

## Traditional Workshop Versus Workshop with Book Clubs

Lucy Calkins can often be heard saying, "The beauty of a workshop is its simplicity." There is a rhythm to a reading workshop that comes from following the same routine each day. After a few weeks, it feels, to those who participate in it, like getting into a good kind of groove. Kids don't get bored because, though the routines are the same each day, the actual work within those routines is new, engaging, and challenging. The workshop provides a liberating sense of consistency, safety, and predictability that students need in order to undertake the challenging academic tasks we're expecting of them, and this makes it a perfect playground (or structure) for establishing book clubs.

You can certainly have a reading workshop that doesn't include book clubs. In a traditional workshop, students usually have more informal conversations about their books in pairs or trios. But for book clubs to be established and to thrive, they need to function within the context of a workshop, because readers will need consistent opportunities and the low-risk environment that a well-established workshop can provide. For many students, engaging in rigorous academic conversation about books is challenging new work.

## Minilesson

Reading workshop almost always starts with a brief whole-class lesson. Students gather in a cozy corner of the room, close to their teacher, to engage in some instruction. This might take the form of an inquiry lesson, a shared reading lesson, or a lesson in which the teacher explicitly demonstrates for the students something new to try. The goal is to keep this lesson clear and brief—no longer than twelve to fifteen minutes—to allow maximum time for students to read on their own and prepare for their book clubs.

In a traditional reading workshop, the minilesson can focus on a variety of things, such as fluency, word solving, and comprehension strategies. We often read and reread picture books, big books, or short texts projected onto a screen to demonstrate some new work students are ready for.

In book clubs, minilessons explicitly address the needs of students as they read for, prepare for, and participate in book clubs. Minilessons focus on establishing book club routines, reading to deepen understanding, preparing for talk, and participating in academic conversations. They also provide an opportunity to explicitly address a common need we see cropping up among the book clubs in our class.

While launching book clubs in a fourth-grade classroom, I noticed that many of the clubs were spending most of their discussions retelling or summarizing the main events that occurred in the chapters they read. So, while working with a couple of those clubs, I paraphrased a particular scene the students had

> ## Teaching TIP
> Since most students are reading chapter books with their book clubs, it is valuable to use chapter books in minilessons as well. This ensures that the teacher's instruction, modeling, and opportunities for practice reflect the level of sophistication required in the books the students are reading.

described and then posed the questions "What did that part make you think?" and, "What seemed particularly important about that scene?" With those questions, students were able to say their idea and then start a discussion based on their *thinking* rather than on *retelling* events. Since I noticed this pattern of summarizing with multiple clubs, I decided to teach the whole class a strategy for shifting from retelling to discussing an idea. I taught the students that, rather than waiting for a teacher to pose a question, they could listen for a summary, paraphrase it briefly, and then ask their book club, "What did that part make you think or wonder?" Whole-group instruction allowed me to design my teaching based on a common need rather than teaching the same lesson to four separate book clubs.

### Independent Reading

Once the minilesson is finished, students head off to independent reading. Multiple studies over decades (Guthrie and Humenick 2004) have shown that students who spend the most time reading make the most progress, so it's essential to maximize the time available for students to do the important work of reading books, jotting their thinking, and talking about their ideas with other readers.

Students learn early on how to make thoughtful decisions about where in the room they'll read so they can be the most productive and have the fewest distractions. You've probably seen classrooms where students are spread out around the room, sitting on the carpet, on beanbag chairs, even tucked into a cozy corner. Students bring all their reading materials with them; this is usually a magazine file or a book box with the books they are reading or planning to read.

In a traditional workshop, a book box might include guided reading books provided by the teacher, books students have chosen from the classroom library, a book or two from the school or public library, and a favorite book from home. Each day students decide which books they'll read and what to jot down that will help them think more deeply about their books.

During book clubs, however, students prioritize their book club book and use independent reading time to read the amount agreed upon by the club. We know that students read at different paces, so students also have a book "on deck"—another book they are reading that they can return to whenever they finish reading their book club assignment.

## Teaching TIP

By providing long, uninterrupted swaths of time for independent reading, we allow students to build ideas across pages, chapters, and even books in a series. As a result of these connections, students are often able to bring more substance to their book club conversation.

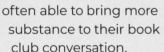

Jotting is often more focused and goal-oriented during a book club. Rather than jotting whatever comes to mind, readers participating in a book club often jot thoughts related to the previous book club discussion or the goal the club members have set for themselves. During a book club discussion on *Number the Stars*, a group of sixth graders realized Lois Lowry repeatedly referred to fairy tales as a way to contrast a fantasy world with the horrors of Nazi Germany. Once the book club members came to this conclusion, they decided to read the next few chapters with this focus, jotting any time they noticed this pattern emerging.

## Transitioning to Talk

After reading independently for twenty to forty minutes (depending on the students' age and the time of year), the class is notified that it's time for talk. In a traditional workshop, this might happen in a variety of ways. In some classrooms, kids head off to a literacy station or center that involves some sort of authentic and engaging practice. Stations could include listening to a book on tape, reading and talking with a partner about a picture book, or developing thinking by writing about it in their reader's notebook.

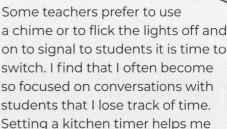

**Teaching TIP**

Some teachers prefer to use a chime or to flick the lights off and on to signal to students it is time to switch. I find that I often become so focused on conversations with students that I lose track of time. Setting a kitchen timer helps me as much as it helps the students.

However, during book clubs, instead of heading to stations or pairing up for partner time, students come together around the room for their book club discussions. For the sake of predictability and routine, each book club meets in the same spot every day. Some clubs convene in the carpeted meeting area where the whole-group lesson takes place, others choose a cluster of desks, while another club camps out on the floor. Students always bring the same materials to meet their book club—a copy of their book, their reader's notebook, and any tools the club is using. (I'll talk more about tools for clubs in Chapter 3: Forming Groups and Launching Book Clubs.)

New routines, such as meeting with a book club, will inevitably lead to new management issues that you'll need to address through explicit teaching. In Samantha Rumley's third-grade classroom, students were often showing up to book club without the materials they needed. "Where's your book?" she would ask them. "Where's your reader's notebook with

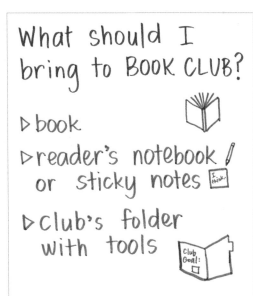

**Figure 1.1**

your thinking?" Once she realized this was a pattern across multiple clubs, she decided the routines weren't automatic enough, and she retaught them. Students practiced doing a mental checklist on their way to their book club: "Do I have my book? My reader's notebook? Our tools?" Samantha even posted a checklist (see Figure 1.1) in the room to remind students what they should bring.

## Time for Reflection and Sharing

After ten to fifteen minutes of discussing the book, another signal cues readers that it's time for a brief reflection back in the meeting area. Students quickly clean up and return to the same spots and sit next to the same person (usually a reading partner) they sat with at the beginning of the workshop.

In a traditional reading workshop, the teacher might highlight a student who tried on today's teaching point or ask all students to reflect on their work toward today's lesson or a larger goal.

During book clubs, Reflect and Share is a time to support students as they acquire the skills needed to sustain productive academic conversations. If I feel that students need to develop a clearer vision of what an engaging book club discussion looks like, I might fishbowl one particular club by placing its members in the center of a circle for the others to observe. I often give the observing students a lens, such as "What do you notice this club does to get the conversation started?" or "What do you see this club doing that helps them *keep* the conversation going?" When I first launch book clubs, I might pose a more fundamental question such

## Teaching TIP

I make myself a list of routines I'll need to teach explicitly and space them out throughout the first unit of study. They include (but aren't limited to) these lessons:

- Finding a rug spot
- Talking with a turn-and-talk partner
- Responding to the signal to turn to the teacher
- Finding an independent spot
- Selecting a club spot
- Remembering what to bring to independent reading and club time

as "What does this book club do that shows us they are listening to each other?" The class observes a book club and names the strategies the group is utilizing. The goal of this inquiry is to get a glimpse of the ways other clubs are functioning and encourage students to reflect on their own work in clubs.

The following chart summarizes the differences I have described between a traditional reading workshop and a reading workshop with book clubs.

## Traditional Workshop Versus a Workshop with Book Clubs

| | TRADITIONAL | WITH BOOK CLUBS |
|---|---|---|
| **Whole-Group Instruction** | Lesson or interactive read-aloud focusing on anything that helps readers: comprehension, fluency, word solving. | Lesson or interactive read-aloud focusing on skills and strategies to support students as they read for, prepare for, and participate in book clubs. |
| **Independent Reading** | Students read texts of their choice, including picture books, magazines, novels, nonfiction books. | Students read their book club text, jotting their thinking as a way to prepare for the conversation. |
| **Talking About Books** | Reading partners read together and talk about their books. | Book clubs meet to engage in academic discourse about their ideas. Ideas are carried over across conversations to build more complex thinking. |
| **Reflect and Share** | Teacher highlights a few students who have tried unit-related work. | Teacher fishbowls a book club or highlights a few book clubs that have tried unit-related work. |

## Preparing Students for Book Clubs Within the Reading Workshop

While the preceding section describes an ideal scenario of a reading workshop, none of this happens on its own. Students won't come to our classroom in September automatically knowing our expectations. We'll teach, reinforce, remind, and reteach each of these expectations until it has become routine and the students rarely look to us to know what to do each day.

A predictable workshop, like the one described in Figure 1.2, is an important structure to put in place early in the year. But any workshop is just the context in which you will teach the real stuff—reading, writing, thinking, and talking. Reading workshop provides a time each day when students can engage in the authentic work of reading texts and talking about their thinking with a book club that will hold them accountable, challenge them, and help them grow across a year. The predictable structure also provides the time we teachers need to observe book clubs at work, assess their strengths and needs, and teach in response to our observations.

| **Whole-Group Instruction** (e.g., Focus Lesson, Inquiry Lesson, Interactive Read-Aloud) (8–12 minutes) | |
|---|---|
| **STUDENTS** | **TEACHER** |
| **Independent Reading** (20–40 minutes) | Teaching small groups and conferring (25–55 minutes) |
| **Talking About Books** (5–15 minutes) | |
| **Reflect and Share** (5 minutes) | |

**Figure 1.2**

An example of a predictable structure for reading workshop. Purple indicates what students are doing. Blue indicates what the teacher is doing. Green indicates what the whole group is doing together.

Once workshop is up and running smoothly, it's time to dig into the work that will serve as a scaffolded bridge to independent book clubs. In the next chapter, we'll explore paths to get kids talking in book-clubby ways.

CHAPTER **2**

## Scaffolding Toward Book Club Conversations

**I**T WAS MY FOURTH YEAR of teaching, and I had just started at a new school in Brooklyn, New York. The school had been working with the Teachers College Reading and Writing Project for a decade, and many of the teachers were familiar with the concept of book clubs. I, on the other hand, was a novice. I had primarily been planning units of study on my own, using what I had done in past years and trying to apply new ideas as I encountered them. I had never tried book clubs before, but the idea excited me. It brought together all the things I valued about instruction—collaboration, authenticity, and student engagement. During a team meeting in January, I listened as my colleagues discussed plans to launch book clubs the following week. As a new teacher at the school, I gathered that setting up book clubs was standard practice and knew my students should have the opportunity to participate in book clubs as well. "I better get this going," I thought to myself. I decided to dive into the deep end.

On the first day of the unit, I handed my second graders copies of a variety of short chapter books and picture books and explained that they would read independently, jot their thoughts, and then gather with their reading groups to discuss. About thirty minutes later, after students had read independently, they gathered in small groups around the room for their first book club meeting. If I'm being honest, mostly what they did was sit and stare at each other. They were aware that they were supposed to be doing *something*, but they weren't sure what that was. One group flipped through the pages of the picture book they had just read and retold the story scene by scene to each other. One group stared at each other awkwardly. Another group discussed recent events that had occurred at recess. One girl started to braid another's hair.

Despite multiple instructional attempts, much of the behavior I observed on the first day continued. After independent reading, the book clubs met around the room with varying levels of success and engagement. As a classroom teacher new to this work, I felt like I needed many more adults in the room to manage the chaos of launching book clubs. Only in retrospect did I see that I had forgotten an essential idea in instruction: the gradual release of responsibility.

Instead of providing the necessary support, I had thrown students into the deep end of book clubs and hoped they would meet productively simply because I had provided them with the opportunity. While opportunity is essential for learning, it is rarely enough. If we're teaching something truly new and challenging and worthwhile, we need to provide a high level of scaffolding early on, then gradually release this support so that students take on more and more over time. It's essential to remember that complex skills take time to develop, and the transfer to independence happens slowly, gradually, with both opportunity and support. Rather than thinking of book clubs as the starting point, we might think of independent book clubs as the long-term goal. When students walk in the door in September, they might not be ready . . . yet. But this doesn't prevent us from putting opportunities and scaffolds in place that will help them build toward this independence.

Whenever I think of the gradual release of responsibility model, I'm reminded of my young son learning to swim. Too small and not yet skilled enough to participate on the pool's swim team, he instead joined "Bubbles," the modified swim team for preschool-aged children. That first summer, he swam laps with a coach ahead of him, pulling his little arms, demonstrating for him how to blow bubbles along the way. Eventually, the coach handed him a faded red kickboard and swam alongside him, reminding him to flutter-kick in order to propel *himself* forward. After two summers of this, he began to swim on his own, with the coach nearby, prompting him to hold his arms in streamline, to kick his feet, and to breathe. For almost two whole summers, the swim coach kept in her mind the long-term goal—swimming laps independently. She considered the scaffolds my son would need to feel success early on and the opportunities he would need to build his (literal) muscles and his confidence. And most importantly, she looked for signs he was ready for the scaffolding to be removed or at least lightened so that he could do more on his own.

Our considerations are the same for book clubs: What are my long-term goals for students? What opportunities will I provide to build their muscles? What scaffolding can I provide so they experience success within these opportunities?

## Interactive Read-Aloud

The gradual release of responsibility model (Pearson and Gallagher 1983) helps us think about our instruction as a progression from heavy to lightened support. As you scaffold your readers toward independence in book clubs, you'll likely find it useful to organize that support in stages of "to," "with," and "by." When students are new to book clubs, they'll need lots of modeling and coaching before moving on to independent practice, so we begin with interactive read-alouds, holding the text and reading it *to* them, in order to significantly lighten their cognitive load. Since students do not need to spend time decoding the text in this stage, they're freed to concentrate on deeper levels of comprehension and on more sophisticated academic talk.

Later, we'll think about ways to lighten our support, reading *with* students until the work of book clubs can eventually be sustained *by* them. But first, let's look at several ways you might scaffold students toward independence, as you read to them during interactive read-alouds.

## What Interactive Read-Aloud IS and What It's NOT

When I think of interactive read-aloud, I try to keep one image crystal clear in my mind. The image is of a parent, sitting on the edge of a child's bed, reading them a favorite book at bedtime. The parent reads and the child listens, forming images of the story in their mind. Both parent and child are enjoying this time together because they are both having an authentic reading experience. The parent might talk about their thinking—expressing concern for Wilbur as the farmers discuss the approaching spring. The child might gasp as they learn something new about Templeton and his conflicting motivations. Either reader, the parent or the child, might interrupt the reading of the text to ask a question or to clarify something. All along, throughout the book, the focus is on meaning, enjoyment, and engagement.

This image is one I try to replicate each time I conduct an interactive read-aloud in a classroom. I want students to interrupt me to ask a question ("Wait! Is he being sincere or sarcastic here? I can't tell!") I want us to swoon together over great lines of writing ("Oh! I just love that line: 'Night came with many stars.'") And I want us to develop some ideas that change as we learn more ("Ira is acting different—he's not listening to his sister anymore.")

Most importantly, I want students to feel a sense of success and engagement as readers. By success I mean I want them to know that they can do the work of reading, which is building meaning across a text. By engagement I mean I want students to experience what it feels like to lose themselves in a story or have their minds blown by a nonfiction book. I know I've got it right when I close the book and a collective moan erupts from the class.

Unfortunately, read-aloud can sometimes lose its magic in today's busy and high-stakes schools. The practice of reading aloud remains, but the method often loses its luster when it's used as an informal assessment to see whether students "got it" or not. If we aren't intentional, read-aloud can become just another opportunity to ask students questions that mimic standardized assessments ("What's the main idea of this section?"). It can feel like a pop quiz in which the teacher asks all the questions and the students provide all the answers, reenacting the predictable pattern of speaking practiced in schools for decades: the teacher asks a question, a student responds, and the teacher evaluates the response.

## Designing Your Interactive Read-Alouds

As you design interactive read-alouds, try to keep a few things in mind to make them engaging and meaningful. First, make sure that participating in an interactive read-aloud *feels* like real reading. So when you're deciding where to stop during the reading to talk about something, try asking yourself the question "What would *I* want to think and talk about?" Try to answer this question not as a teacher but as a real reader, looking for the parts where you're creating a particularly vivid picture in your mind, or having a strong emotional reaction, or formulating or revising an idea. These same parts where you would naturally want to stop and talk to someone are also great opportunities for students to stop, think, and talk with a partner.

However, be cautious with this. Though selecting spots where we, as readers, have things to say can be a great way to open conversations, it might also lead to a common pitfall of interactive read-alouds: leading students to arrive at the same thinking we have. If you think you know the answer or there is just one "right" answer, try not to even ask the question. For example, if you're noticing that Opal (*Because of Winn-Dixie*) is showing how lonely she is, you don't want to ask, "How is Opal feeling?" and hope the students come to the same conclusion you did. Asking students a question we think we know the answer to conditions them to play Guess What the Teacher Thinks. Instead of asking a question, share your own thinking through a think-aloud. That might sound like this: "Opal must feel so lonely. That's probably why she's so desperate to keep this dog."

On the other hand, if there are multiple possible answers, try to suggest that in your question by using language that implies ambiguity. Instead of saying, "*Why is* Opal begging her dad for this dog?" you might say, "*What might be some reasons* Opal is begging for this dog?" The switch from "Why is" (which implies a single answer) to "What might be some reasons" (which implies many answers) is an important one for students. It implicitly suggests that readers will come to different conclusions and that they should expect to have a variety of ideas.

You can also try to use tentative language. "Is" is definitive. "Why is Opal sad?" suggests there is a correct answer. "Why might Opal be sad?" suggests we aren't sure and we are trying to figure it out. It's tentative. It's just a possibility.

Lastly, keep the concepts of scaffolding and gradual release of responsibility in mind. We want to provide a balance of think-alouds (demonstrating our own thinking) and turn-and-talks (opportunities for students to practice with support). If we ask students to turn and talk during every stopping place, we're not providing models for more sophisticated levels of thinking. On the other hand, if all we do is model, we're not providing students with opportunities to take on new ways of thinking. As you plan, anticipate places to stop, and adjust the level of scaffolding in direct response to your students.

The following chart provides four concepts to consider as you plan your stopping points for an interactive read-aloud.

| DESIGNING AN INTERACTIVE READ-ALOUD | |
|---|---|
| **Authenticity** | ■ What are the parts that I, as a proficient reader, have thoughts about and reactions to?<br>■ What are some things readers might think and talk about within these parts? |
| **Multiples Possibilities** | ■ What are some ways . . . ? |
| **Tentative Thinking** | ■ What are you thinking about ___?<br>■ Why might . . . ?<br>■ How might . . . ?<br>■ What might be some ways . . . ? |
| **Intensity of Scaffolding** | ■ Heavy: I'm thinking . . . I'm noticing . . . I'm wondering . . .<br>■ Medium: What are you thinking/noticing/ wondering about ___?<br>■ Light: What are you thinking?. |

## Whole-Class Conversation

Interactive read-aloud is an essential method for supporting student discourse around books, but alone, it isn't necessarily enough of a bridge for students who are learning how to participate in book clubs. In addition to a lively interactive read-aloud each day, whole-class conversation is a highly scaffolded first step. These two components, interactive read-aloud and whole-class conversation, work together to provide students with the experience of using discourse to make meaning of a text in a group setting.

Whole-class conversation goes by many names, but essentially it involves a class of students sitting together to discuss a book they've recently heard during interactive read-aloud. Just as interactive read-aloud mimics the work proficient readers do while reading, whole-class conversation provides the experience of readers discussing a text and their ideas about it in a way similar to what smaller book clubs do. Imagine that you and a group of your friends have all just read the same newspaper article or novel. What would you want to talk about? What ideas do you already have to bring to the table? What's worth exploring together? These are the questions that drive our work during whole-class conversation and all discussions about text.

This method is a great entry point into book clubs for a few important reasons. First, it provides an opportunity for flexible scaffolding. Whole-class conversation allows us to be present for the conversation in its entirety, frontloading students with a topic worthy of discussion. We remain careful observers during the conversation, providing and removing scaffolding as the students need it. After the conversation, we can lead students in a reflection about how the conversation went. What was successful about today's discussion? What might we need to be aware of or to work on during our next conversation?

Second, whole-class conversation provides a common experience for the entire class of students. In every classroom, in every school, students arrive with a wide variety of experiences observing and participating in social and academic conversations. Some students sit around the dinner table each night discussing recent news events with their families. Some students observe those conversations but are asked to sit quietly while adults do the talking. Some students participate in more social conversations about weekend events or sports. And some students are steeped in storytelling language, hearing family lore recounted over and over again. Regardless of our students' prior experience, it is helpful to provide multiple opportunities for them to witness and participate in academic conversations.

Lastly, whole-class conversation is an essential entry point because it serves as an authentic replication of what students will experience outside of elementary and middle school. In upper grades, college classes, and even future work situations, students will probably sit around a table and be expected to put their ideas forward, listen to their peers' ideas, and revise their previous thinking. And more than likely, they'll be evaluated (officially or unofficially) on their ability to do so. Learners will need to be able to pose questions, explore each other's answers, and come to consensus (or not). If this is the work students will most likely do in higher education and in the workplace, it makes sense to provide them with these experiences early.

## Launching Whole-Class Conversations

A whole-class conversation often starts immediately after a read-aloud. Ask the students to move into a circle where they can see each other. It turns out that just forming a circle rather than sitting in rows can create a shift in students' behavior during the conversation. Often, students are used to facing and responding directly to the teacher when speaking, so try to shift that dynamic physically first. Even when students are used to turning and talking to a partner, they often "report back" (or "share out") to the teacher as a whole class. While it can be a little cumbersome at first—forming a circle with twenty or twenty-five students usually involves pushing a desk or table out of the way—sitting in a circle sends the implicit message that students should talk to *each other* and not the teacher, which is one of the new behaviors you're trying to cultivate.

You don't want to assume students know your expectations for engaging in a whole-class conversation, so in the beginning, establish very clear guidelines. Here are the three guidelines I've found most helpful in getting started.

### GUIDELINES FOR WHOLE-CLASS CONVERSATION

1. **When you have something to say, you can speak without being called on.** You don't have to raise your hand.

2. **Only one voice should be speaking at a time**. If someone else is speaking, it's not your turn yet.

3. **All eyes should be on the speaker,** even if that means you need to turn your body or your head.

Even though you'll name all three guidelines for the class before you start the first whole-class conversation, it's not guaranteed that students will know how to follow them. Speaking in a group without raising hands is incredibly challenging for students who have spent years learning to wait to be called on. However, after a day or two, students quickly adapt to this new expectation and can flexibly move between raising their hands in some contexts and participating more spontaneously in others.

Learning how to start (and stop) speaking within a larger group is challenging, and I'll address those predictable challenges a bit later. You can expect that students will approximate the guidelines with varying degrees of proficiency and that you'll need to work on them throughout the year.

One other physical factor that helps with the shift to whole-class conversation is the location of the teacher. If you place yourself as a part of the circle, students may still direct their attention to you. To avoid this, ask them to close the circle while you sit outside of it. When this setup is new to students, you might notice that a few of them will still turn their bodies and direct their talk to you. Here are a few strategies to shift this behavior.

You might try *not* to make eye contact with the students. This feels strange and awkward at first because we are used to facilitating, if not leading, the conversation. Students will look to us when they respond. But part of what we're trying to do in a whole-class conversation is to teach students how to talk to and listen to each other rather than to a teacher. Instead of looking at the speakers, try to take a transcript of the talk, jotting down students' ideas and taking note of which students are speaking. If a student turns their body to direct their comment to you, you might nudge them to "tell the group" or "speak to the class." Changing students' behavior about whom they speak to when discussing their ideas is often the first predictable teaching you'll do here.

Getting started with academic conversations can be another challenging part of establishing effective book club interactions. Initiating a conversation that is meaningful, inviting, and intellectually demanding takes work and skill. But it is a skill that can be practiced and honed. Even when generating topics worth discussion, it's helpful to think about the gradual release of responsibility. How might we provide models, then support students in some guided practice, before eventually releasing them to independent book clubs?

Early in the year, you might generate a few possible discussion topics from which students may select. After reading, put three ideas or topics on the dry erase board and let the class vote on which one they want to talk about. By doing this, you provide some models of rich discussion topics for students. I used to craft questions that students could answer through their conversations, but then I noticed that in my own book club, adults rarely began a discussion by posing a formal question to the group. More often, they put forward a topic or a tentative idea they wanted to explore with the group. One member of my book club might start by saying something like this: "I was thinking about that ending. I was questioning whether the character really believed what she was saying there." In this same way, you can suggest a few topics or ideas that are worth discussing, letting students be responsible for paving a path into the discussion.

For example, after reading *Fox* by Margaret Wild (2006), I posted these three topics on the board:

1. "The scream of anguish or despair"

2. How Magpie changed

3. The ending

Regardless of which topic the students select, they will end up discussing the complicated relationships between the three main characters, the uncertainty of change, or the motivations and backstory of the characters. With this heavy scaffold, I'm doing some of the work of providing topics worth discussing. At the same time, I'm implicitly showing students that there are a number of things worth diving deep into in *any* book we talk about, and I'm modeling how to generate a conversation-starting idea. Of course, I could also teach this explicitly by gradually building a chart, such as the one shown in Figure 2.1, over several interactions.

A slightly lighter scaffold would be to ask the class for a few suggested topics or ideas worth discussing and allow students to select one. While this can be challenging in the very beginning of the year, with a few weeks (or a couple of months) of teacher modeling, students are usually ready to provide some options. The student-suggested topics provide us teachers with a little formative assessment as well.

**Figure 2.1**

What kinds of things are they thinking about? What kinds of topics do they currently think are worth discussing? This information helps us make decisions about whether to provide or remove scaffolds.

There is an added benefit of listing possible topics and selecting one before the conversation begins. Many times, students need time to think through the topic or idea before talking about it. Knowing the topic, even just a few minutes ahead of time, allows students to "prepare" for the conversation. Sometimes that preparation comes in the form of a silent minute or two just to think. "What might you say about the relationship between Fox and Magpie?" you might say. "Take a minute and think to yourself." This gives internal processors a chance to quietly explore their own thinking. Other times, you might invite students to talk to their shoulder partner (turn-and-talk partner) before your whole-class conversation. This gives external processors an opportunity to figure out what they think before sharing with the class. And sometimes you might do both, providing thinking time and partner-talk time before the whole-class conversation begins.

When students are consistently generating multiple topics worth discussing, then you have enough evidence that they no longer need a scaffold. Instead of listing a few topics on the board and voting, you could just pose the question "Who can get us started with our discussion today?" Consider their responses a formative assessment as well and be prepared to respond with scaffolding as needed. If you hear students consistently launching the conversation with a retelling, you could provide a heavier scaffold again. Or provide some more explicit instruction around generating ideas worth discussing. It's also helpful to explicitly name your process and the decisions you're making as you come up with ideas. See Figure 2.2 for a summary of tips that help launch a successful whole-class conversation.

Figure 2.2

| TIPS FOR LAUNCHING WHOLE-CLASS CONVERSATION |
| --- |
| ■ Have students sit in a circle. |
| ■ Establish guidelines. (Share without waiting to be called on. One voice at a time. Look at the speaker.) |
| ■ Sit outside the circle, take notes, and act as a nonparticipating observer as much as possible. |
| ■ Scaffold choosing topic to launch conversation. |

## Sustaining and Developing
## Whole-Class Conversations

I'm the kind of cook who is hopelessly tethered to a recipe. I read and reread each step at least three times before starting, unable to hold any more information in my mind than my current step. Sometimes, even in the midst of the chop or stir, I return to the step in the recipe, reading to make sure I got it right. I am almost never able to anticipate the next step, and I am definitely not able to be responsive to the task in front of me. If the recipe comes out too saucy or sweet or dry, I serve it anyway with a shrug and a smile. "Guess it's not a good recipe," I assure myself, despite finding it on a "best recipes" list.

My husband, Alex, is on the opposite end of this spectrum. He can taste something at a restaurant and recreate some version of it weeks later, improvising with whatever ingredients we happen to have. He never follows a recipe to a tee but instead considers it a mere suggestion. He finds it confining to follow some other chef's directions, preferring to look in our fridge, grab what's there, and taste along the way.

After watching him cook for a few years, I realized that he approaches cooking in a way I hadn't yet learned. He anticipates challenges and expects that he will need to respond accordingly. Too sweet? He adds some spice or acid. Sauce too runny? He adds a bit of flour or cornstarch. Not flavorful enough? He searches for a sauce or stock to add depth.

My hunch is that many of us approach whole-class conversations in the way that I approach a recipe. We follow the prescribed steps, we do what we've learned, and when things go "wrong," we give up. We might think, "I tried it, but this class isn't ready." Or "We did it a few times, but there are too many kids who are just learning to speak English." Or "There are too many strong personalities in my class for this to work."

But teaching whole-class conversation actually requires that we approach our students the way my husband approaches cooking. We must anticipate challenges and expect that we will need to respond accordingly. The good news is that there are some predictable challenges you can prepare for. And it turns out that they are not, in fact, signs that your class isn't ready. It's quite the opposite. These predictable challenges are opportunities to teach and support students' growth toward independent book clubs.

## Predictable Challenges and Possible Responses

**Challenge #1: Students don't talk, or there is a lot of silence.**

- **OPTION #1:** Wait one to two full minutes before stepping in to correct this. It is not our job to remove awkward silence. Many teachers are uncomfortable with any silence at all and leave no time for actual thinking. When we constantly step in to fill the silence, we foster a learned dependency in students. In other words, we implicitly send the message that the teacher is responsible for doing the work.

- **OPTION #2:** Use turn-and-talk as a verbal rehearsal for a whole-group share. Sometimes the issue is not that the students don't have anything to say. It's that they aren't yet comfortable sharing their ideas with the larger group. By allowing students to rehearse their thinking with a partner, we provide more safety and scaffolding. Ask students to turn to their partner and talk about what they're thinking. Then, listen to partnerships and ask a student (maybe a more reluctant student) to share their thinking in order to jump start the conversation again.

- **OPTION #3:** Step out of the role of the observer briefly and participate in the conversation by sharing your own thinking or wondering. Be careful not to dominate the conversation, but instead act as a proficient member of the book club. Other times, a handful of students can serve as models of productive academic conversations.

**Challenge #2: Students talk over each other or don't listen to each other.**

- **OPTION #1:** Teach nonverbal communication. It can be tempting to introduce tools such as a "talking stick" or playing cards that students need to use in order to speak. While this may solve one challenge (students talking at the same time), it introduces a new challenge (utilizing a prop). The teacher still needs to teach students how to use and manage the prop, and in the end, they still haven't learned authentic ways to participate in group discussions. Instead, think about the ways adults enter into an informal group conversation. Teach students to communicate when they are trying to enter a conversation by sitting up, leaning forward, and taking a breath, visually indicating they have something to say. Teach students to look for those who are trying to enter into a conversation and to invite them in by saying, "It looks like you have something to say," or "Did you want to say something?"

- **OPTION #2:** Slow the conversation down by prompting with something like this: "Who can respond to what she just said?" Often, shifting students' thinking or behavior requires us to raise our level of support by taking something implicit and naming it explicitly. Rather than assuming students know they should be responding to each other, I make this expectation explicit by pausing the conversation and giving students a second to think about whether their comment builds on or shifts away from what has just been said. Another option is to pause and ask, "Did that build onto what she said, or is that a new idea?" If it's a new idea, I "rewind" the conversation and ask the students to try it again, this time responding to the previous comment. In traditional school settings, students learn through experience that they will be asked questions by a teacher and that it is their role to raise their hand and share their thinking. Because of this model, many students might find it new and challenging to shift their participation away from merely *sharing* an idea to *responding to* someone else's idea. In early childhood development, we often see two children sitting together, one with a pail and one with a shovel but neither playing or interacting with the other. We call this parallel play (Parten 1933). In the beginning of the year, whole-class conversations often resemble this kind of play, with one student sharing their idea and then another student sharing an unrelated idea. We are trying to shift students to view conversations as a *building* of ideas and a collective construction of understanding rather than as a "share out" or *reporting* of ideas.

### Challenge #3: A handful of students dominate the conversation, and/or a handful of students do not speak.

- **OPTION #1:** As needed, teach a small group of students who are dominating the conversation to use their fingers to monitor how many times they are speaking within each conversation. Each time they speak, they put up a finger on their hand. This is a way for students to keep track of their own participation. If there is a group of eighteen to twenty-four students, and a certain student has spoken four or five times, that student probably should make space for others to share their thinking. As with any of the predictable challenges, the goal is to teach students to monitor their own behavior and develop authentic strategies that serve them inside and outside of the school setting. Rather than monitoring for students, it is helpful to teach them ways to check on themselves and to be aware of their own participation.

- **OPTION #2:** Begin the conversation with a turn-and-talk. Listen in on the internal processors, the introverts, and the students who are less willing to share. Offer those students an opportunity to "launch" the discussion. Each of us lands somewhere on a continuum from extrovert to introvert. Many of us figure out what we are going to say while we're talking. We don't need to know our idea beforehand but instead find it helpful to "talk it out." Others of us need think time. We can't begin to speak until we have had time to process in our own minds and compose our idea. We have students in our class on both ends and all along this spectrum as well.

- **OPTION #3:** Fishbowl a conversation. Form an inner circle of students who will participate in a brief conversation and an outer circle of students who will observe and give feedback. It's sometimes helpful for the students who are verbal processors to observe students who need more think time and to notice their behavior. Other times you might have the students who are internal processors sit on the outside and provide feedback.

## Approximation

We know that the way we learn anything—cooking, swimming, reading— is by doing it over and over with a mentor (a more proficient other) who provides feedback. There is no way to learn to swim without getting in the water. There is no way to learn to cook without standing in front of a stove and tasting the sauce. There is no way to learn how to talk without engaging in a meaningful conversation. The one and only way anyone ever becomes skilled at discussing books is by discussing books. If we "wait until students are ready" to provide them with opportunities, we are actually just depriving them of the early experiences that are critical.

I am reminded of this every time I talk with my own young kids. As parents, or aunts, or uncles, we understand that three-year-olds will insist on participating in whatever way they can. They will interrupt with an unrelated declaration ("I like cheese now!") or interject with a story that is only loosely related to what was being discussed. We might even engage the toddler with a question such as "You got new goggles, didn't you? What was it like to swim with goggles?" Even before they can answer in whole sentences, we expect some sort of response. At home we see all these interactions as chances to model conversation, to provide opportunities for the child to approximate, and to coach and provide informal feedback.

This same idea—of providing opportunities that allow for approximations—applies in our classrooms. In order to improve, students will need multiple opportunities to use what they currently know about talk and gradually acquire new, and increasingly academic, conversation skills. A colleague of mine, Suzanne Fisher, described an early whole-class conversation in a kindergarten classroom. Students sat in a circle discussing *Sheila Rae, the Brave*. "I think Louise is really brave," a girl with two long braids said to the group. "You know how to braid your own hair!?!?" exclaimed another girl sitting across the circle. Suzanne recalls this story, laughing about the predictable challenges she faces every year when she introduces this work to students. She takes these challenges not as a sign that her young readers aren't *ready* to talk to each other about books but as a sign that they *are* ready. Ready for opportunity. Ready to approximate. Ready for feedback and coaching.

## Read-Aloud Book Clubs

While whole-class conversation is incredibly supportive and highly scaffolded, it doesn't necessarily prepare students to function in independent books clubs right away. It does provide them with the vision and experience of participating in an academic conversation, and that is essential. In this section, we continue to think about how to gradually lighten the scaffold so that we, the teachers, control and facilitate less and the students control and facilitate more.

One way to do this is with read-aloud book clubs. We begin as we did before with a meaningful and engaging experience through interactive read-aloud. But then, rather than remaining in the meeting area for a whole-class conversation, students break off into groups of four or five around the room to have a discussion. This provides them an experience of meeting with a club while also allowing the teacher to set them up for successful conversations about the book.

We orchestrate this by providing a rich interactive read-aloud that builds toward complex ideas. What happens at the end of the read-aloud turns out to be just as important as what happens throughout. If we finish a read-aloud and there is not much more to say or we have inadvertently built consensus around a single idea, sustaining an additional five- to ten-minute discussion afterward will be challenging. But if we end a read-aloud with burning questions or tentative ideas, we've provided a launching pad for student discussion. Before we send students off to their read-aloud book clubs, we can provide the same kind of scaffolding we did before the whole-class conversation. At first, we might suggest three topics and ask that each book club decide which one they will discuss. Later, we might take three suggestions from the class and allow each club to select one. As we build toward independence, we might just say, "Decide what you'll talk about today," and send the groups off to begin their discussions.

While it's possible to sustain a conversation for a long while, I find that it's helpful to start small. Usually in the beginning of this work, five minutes of discussion will do it. The long-term goal is to build up to a longer, more in-depth discussion, but I've found that it's helpful to keep it short and manageable as students build their stamina and skill.

While students meet with their book clubs, select one or two clubs to listen in on and coach from the sidelines. I think of this as being much like the "scrimmage" part of my son's soccer practice. The goal of the scrimmage is to provide players an opportunity to put into use all they've learned from that day's drills and from previous practices. The coaches don't stop the scrimmage to offer instruction. Instead, they run alongside the players, or coach them from the sidelines. "Formation!" they might say, reminding the players not to clump around the ball, just as they practiced in the drill twenty minutes earlier. Similarly, since these initial read-aloud book clubs have only about five minutes to talk, I don't want to interrupt the flow of the conversation. "Who can add on to Damien's point?" I might suggest, reminding students to build onto an idea rather than moving on to a new one, just as we practiced in whole-class conversation. (We'll take a deeper look at how to use the group's conversation as an assessment to inform our teaching in Chapter 4: Utilizing Talk as an Assessment.)

When you're ready, gather everyone back together as a whole group to reflect on what went well and what was challenging. Students will usually identify the issues themselves, setting a clear path for the needed instruction ahead. They'll need to learn how to negotiate four or five voices. They'll want to figure out how to get started when nobody initiates the conversation. They'll notice a member of the club dominating, or another member of the club who doesn't seem to participate at all.

The opportunity to talk is beneficial, but without reflection, students won't necessarily use the opportunities to grow and change and build their skills. A reflection, even a brief one once in a while, helps students develop a sense of ownership and offers us, the teachers, some information that can inform our future teaching.

Through interactive read-alouds, whole-class conversations, and eventually read-aloud book clubs, you'll notice that, gradually, students are playing a more active role and you're facilitating less and less. These are signs that kids are ready for some more independence. In Chapter 3, we'll focus on the other decisions you'll make and routines you'll establish throughout the workshop that make book clubs not just possible, but successful.

# Forming Groups and Launching Book Clubs

**I** F YOU'VE EVER TRIED to get a three-year-old dressed in the morning, you've probably engaged in a struggle over decision-making and control. Three-year-olds are notorious for rejecting clothes over an itchy tag or a too-long sleeve or a tight collar. When children eventually start dressing themselves, usually at around four or five years old, they often emerge from their bedrooms in outfits that cause us some embarrassment. Clashing patterns, too many layers, backwards shirts, mismatched socks. But we hand over this responsibility with an eye to the long-term benefit—having children who can select clothing and dress themselves rather than relying on us.

Perhaps you've felt similar struggles as you try to establish routines in your classroom. With each decision we make and each routine we put in place, we ask ourselves, "How much control do I need to have over this decision? What parts of this could students decide for themselves?" And most importantly, "What are the benefits and challenges of each option?"

When we hand over control and teach kids to make decisions for themselves, they often don't make the choices *we* would have them make. They make a partial attempt rather than a perfect one. However, approximations are often where the most learning happens.

We, the teachers, will also make mistakes and course-correct. After all, you might be launching book clubs for the first time and need a chance to reflect on how things are going and what you might want to change in response to how your students are doing. Or you might be a veteran who is introducing book clubs to students who have never been given this much choice and independence before. The more room we all have for new work, the more we'll mess up, which leads to more opportunities for growth.

For each routine we teach to set up effective book clubs, we have a continuum of options ranging from high teacher support to increased student independence. Luckily, there isn't just one right way to run book clubs. Each decision you make has its own benefits and challenges, and you'll need to take into consideration the needs of the wide range of students you have as well as your own needs as a teacher. The following sections will help you consider the choices you have while forming book clubs, determining when and how they meet, and supporting students as they develop an identity as a club.

## Forming Flexible Groups

In the world outside of school, book clubs form for a variety of reasons and in a variety of ways. Some clubs form because there is a single book a handful of people want to discuss. Some clubs form for social purposes and stay together for years, even decades. Other clubs are formed for more professional or academic reasons—a study group that needs support with a challenging text or a company that wants to build some common experiences or knowledge around a topic.

In the classroom, there are also a variety of ways book clubs form, and they can easily change across a year. I tend to keep book clubs together for at least a month so that students can develop a relationship with each other and build some habits together. Since our long-term aim is to provide students with more control and autonomy, our methods for forming groups often evolve to reflect this goal.

## Grouping by Text Level Bands

One way to provide students with a high level of scaffolding in their book clubs is to group them by reading level. Texts at different levels place very different demands on students, so you can create leveled book club groups in much the same way you would form guided reading groups. Decades of research has shown us that it is best for students to read with a high level of accuracy and with deep comprehension (Allington and Gabriel 2011). And since text levels vary so greatly at earlier levels, you'll want to ensure that students are all reading texts they can access.

One year, in a third-grade classroom, my coteacher and I launched book clubs after we reformed our guided reading groups based on midyear assessments. After introducing the book *Houndsley and Catina* to one book club, I asked the students to read the rest of the chapters on their own and meet in two days to discuss the book. Students had been discussing books together within each interactive read-aloud, so they had experiences that prepared them to meet independently with their book clubs.

I find organizing book clubs by text level to be especially useful in younger grades or where there are drastic differences between reading levels. This is also important when students are reading a year or more below grade level. If we are going to accelerate their growth as readers, we need to ensure that students are reading texts well within their control.

The benefit of grouping students by approximate reading level is that it allows for high teacher support. We determine who gets assigned to specific book clubs and therefore can provide the clubs with choices of books we know they can read independently or with light support from us. The challenge with this type of grouping is that students have little input in the club's formation, so they may not be as invested in the group itself. You can use this option when it's essential that students are matched to text levels.

I'm always wary of forming book clubs by text level. I worry it might feel too teacher directed. I worry readers won't experience enough choice and sense of purpose. But once the groups are formed, I remember that, as with all teaching, the key lies in the delivery. I can introduce book clubs in a way that prioritizes compliance and procedures, rules and consequences—"Here's what will happen when your book club gets together,"—or I can introduce book clubs in a way that feels like a special invitation into the literacy club, like a doorway to a back room of a familiar restaurant. I lean in and practically whisper, "You get to meet with your book clubs a few times a week and talk about all of your thoughts."

In my experience, even when I've made the decision about how to group students, I have many other ways to offer them choices, to help them feel the specialness of being a part of a literary club, and to develop their sense of agency. If you recognize that this type of book club grouping is founded in a high level of teacher support, then as with any heavy scaffold, you can compensate by intentionally increasing choice, flexibility, and independence throughout the year.

## Grouping by Student Interest

As students become more strategic and can tackle texts at higher reading levels, you have more flexibility with grouping. Another way you might form groups is by student interest. Some teachers use interest surveys or individual reading conferences to figure out the genres, authors, and topics their students are interested in reading together. Based on students' responses, the teacher forms book clubs around these interests. Phoebe Markle, a fourth-grade teacher, invited her students to fill out a reading interest survey in the middle of the year. After analyzing their responses, she formed one club of students who wanted to read sports biographies, another club that wanted to read the graphic novel series *The Bad Guys*, and a third club that wanted to read Jason Reynolds books. Forming clubs based on students' responses allowed Phoebe to take into account students' own preferences as well as her knowledge of their personalities and needs as readers.

The beauty of forming book clubs based on common interest is that it most closely resembles how book clubs form in the real world, outside of school. We get recommendations from friends, and we start to discover our shared interests and preferences. The challenge in providing this level of choice, however, is that we cannot guarantee that all students are matched to texts they can read, and, though the group's thinking can support the students' understanding of challenging texts, it can only do so up to a point. For example, sixth grader Isaias was able to stretch his ability to read a text level higher than usual with the help of twice-weekly book club discussions and support from his teacher. However, when he attempted to read a book that was more than a year beyond his independent ability, he quickly became frustrated and disengaged—despite his supportive book club members. The book's complex structure and literary language posed challenges that even a rich discussion was not able to alleviate, and Isaias abandoned the book altogether.

Book clubs based on interest can energize a classroom. You'll know book clubs are really humming when the passions and interests of one club start to spread like wildfire around to the other clubs. Years ago, when graphic novels first became popular, I observed a fifth-grade class during book clubs. One club had decided to read the first book of the Amulet series, and after a week, other clubs were begging to do the same. Soon, multiple clubs were on a waitlist to read the book, while others began branching out to other graphic novel series while they waited.

## Grouping by Managed or Open Choice

As students become older and develop the skills that help them become more independent, you can provide structures that allow them to make more decisions. For example, when it comes to forming book clubs, you can provide managed choices, in which you select five to seven titles and students form groups by choosing ones that interests them. Book clubs based on interest in a title or series might stay together or reform for the next book.

Some teachers hand over even more responsibility by employing open-choice, rather than managed-choice, grouping. They invite students to suggest titles for the book clubs. During each "round" of book clubs, five to six students propose a book, and the rest of the students select which club they will join.

The challenges of providing this much autonomy are similar to the challenges of providing any choice at all; they are just amplified. Our students will make choices we don't necessarily agree with. They will select texts we consider to be of lower quality, or texts we didn't enjoy or haven't read yet.

This model also poses challenges in terms of timing. One book club might finish *The City of Ember*'s graphic novel in two days, while another book club takes two weeks to finish *The Stars Beneath Our Feet*. While the differences in timing occur no matter how you group students, flexible grouping poses additional challenges if students want to regroup. It's helpful to have a few checkpoints within each unit at which students can select new texts and form new book clubs.

The benefits of this much choice and responsibility often reveal themselves through the students' sense of engagement and agency. This model is especially appealing to students, since they are responsible both for generating ideas for books and for selecting which ones they want to read. Knowing they will eventually have a turn to propose a book title, students start reading with a different lens: "Would this be a good book to read with a book club?" Some students volunteer to reread a familiar book because they know they'll experience it differently and develop richer ideas and understandings by talking about it with a group. In one eighth-grade class, students decided to start a class list of books they wanted to read and used that collective list to form book clubs. Students started showing up at the door each day with a book in hand, saying, "This is the kind of book I need a book club for."

That sense of not just *having*, but *needing* a book club is what we're really going for here. We want students to feel that while they might thoroughly enjoy reading a book on their own, they gain something more by talking about it with others. By gradually placing responsibility in the hands of students, they start to feel the sense of agency that can transform book clubs from a mere routine into a meaningful and necessary ritual.

I always think back to a third-grade class I once cotaught. After two weeks of book clubs, Edgar approached me with his book in hand. "Can my book club meet after school? Like at someone's house?" That's when I knew things were really working—when a student saw book clubs not as something that happened at a certain time of day but as a part of who he could be in the world.

Whatever way you choose to form clubs, think of it as a temporary formation—in terms of both the members of the groups and the way the groups are formed. Students' strengths evolve at different rates, so you'll need to reassess and reform book clubs at multiple points throughout the year. Over time, students will become more independent as you hand off more of the responsibility and move them increasingly closer to experiencing the authentic ways book clubs form outside of school.

## Book Club Grouping Options

| GROUPING | BENEFITS | CHALLENGES |
|---|---|---|
| **By Text Level Bands** | ■ Students are matched to texts they can access.<br>■ Groups stay together for a month or more, providing time for group identities to form. | ■ Text level is prioritized over student interest.<br>■ Student choice is reduced. |
| **By Student Interest** | ■ Students' interests and preferences are taken into account.<br>■ Groups are highly flexible and may form and reform often. | ■ Students may not be matched to texts at appropriate levels.<br>■ Groups may need to be formed and reformed often. |
| **By Managed or Open Choice** | ■ Groups experience the highest level of student choice and autonomy and ownership over book clubs | ■ Students may not be matched to texts at appropriate levels.<br>■ Groups may need to be formed and reformed often, affording clubs less time to cultivate relationships. |

## Scheduling Book Clubs

You probably haven't heard a colleague say, "We just didn't find time for math this month," or "I didn't have time to read any books to my students this year." When practices are essential, we don't just hope to find time—we make time. Because book clubs are crucial, we can't leave it to chance or schedule it only when we have "extra" time. For book clubs to be effective, they need to be a regular and predictable part of the reading workshop so that students get into habits and know what to expect. Book clubs need to be so predictable that even when there's a substitute, reading workshop and book clubs can still run. For this to happen, you'll need to make decisions about how to schedule book clubs. Not only will you need to decide, you'll need to explicitly teach and coach students until the schedule runs without you.

The reading workshop schedule shown in Chapter 1 (Figure 1.2) always provides time for students to meet and talk, and within that structure, there are decisions you'll need to make. One of those decisions is when and how frequently your book clubs will meet.

## Teacher-Centered Schedule

One option that provides a high level of support is to create a schedule built around your own availability. Just as you might schedule guided reading groups with the aim of meeting with two to three groups a day, you can schedule book clubs in a way that allows you to be present when a book club meets. You might post a weekly schedule, like the one in Figure 3.1, on the wall or announce each day which groups will meet and in what order.

This scheduling method is especially helpful for young students or students who are completely new to book clubs. Students get the experience of meeting regularly (two times a week or so) with a book club, and you can ensure you're present when the book clubs meet to support their conversations. If your teaching is aimed at building the groups' independence, this highly supportive schedule serves as a bridge to more student autonomy later in the year.

The challenge with this level of support is that, by always being present, we run the risk of over-scaffolding and getting in the way of experiences students need to develop independence with book clubs. In our desire to help groups experience success, we often unintentionally end up facilitating the conversation rather than observing and teaching students to facilitate it themselves. We might start the discussion with our own question rather than teaching students how to develop their questions. To make sure this schedule is a temporary scaffold, we need to be aware of and flexible about the scale of our help.

| Monday | Tuesday | Wednesday | Thursday | Friday |
|--------|---------|-----------|----------|--------|
| Club A | Club D | Club B | Club E | Club C |
| Club B | Club C | Club A | Club D | Club F |

**Figure 3.1: Sample Book Club Schedule**
This teacher used this schedule to meet with six book clubs across the week, prioritizing her time with groups that needed more support.

## Daily Meetings or Twice-Weekly Meetings

Another scheduling option that provides predictability is for all book clubs to meet every day simultaneously. I used to think that meeting every day was too often for a book club. How could members read enough to justify meeting and talking every day? That was before I watched the fifth-grade classes at Mason Crest Elementary School do just this. Stacey Duff, one of the school's literacy coaches, reported a huge increase in the time students spent reading, and not just during reading workshop. Students asked to bring their books to lunch and recess. Parents emailed to say they had never seen their kids read this much at home. It turned out that the students actually changed their reading behaviors in response to this rigorous schedule. In other words, they rose to the challenge. In addition to possibly increasing students' reading volume, meeting every day gets all the students (and us, their teachers) into the routine of participating in their book clubs.

Another option is for book clubs to meet every other day. For example, book clubs meet to talk on Tuesday and Thursday. On Monday, Wednesday, and Friday, they have an extended independent reading block or some time to write about their thinking as a way to prepare for or reflect on their book club conversations.

Both scheduling options provide predictability, which helps students anticipate and prepare for their book club discussions. When book clubs decide how much of the book they want to read, they'll first take into consideration how many days they have until their next meeting.

What's challenging about book clubs all meeting at the same time and on the same days is that it's impossible for you to support all of the clubs simultaneously. You'll only be able to listen in, teach, and coach one or two book clubs each day, which means the other book clubs will rely on their current skills and level of independence—in other words, they'll *approximate* book clubs.

The good news is that these approximations (while they might drive you crazy at first) will be exactly what allows students to learn and grow. The club that struggles to come up with anything to talk about will be more receptive to your teaching about generating talk-worthy ideas! The club that is dominated by a single student will be very interested in your lesson on making space for all voices during a conversation! As we always tell our students, mistakes help us grow.

## Club-Managed Schedule

The ultimate level of independence and choice is for the book clubs to decide on their own how often they need to meet. Some book clubs find that meeting for five to ten minutes each day helps them understand the text better and increases their volume of reading. Other clubs prefer longer stretches of time to read with less frequent meeting times. This is often helpful with longer chapter books that develop more slowly. In order to make decisions about how often the book clubs will meet, students need opportunities for self-reflection, time for trial and error, and feedback from you.

Students benefit from this amount of agency and choice because it most closely mimics the behavior of book clubs outside of school and allows them to tailor the club's schedule to their particular needs. A neighborhood book club might meet monthly to discuss a novel they've finished, while a group of teachers might choose to meet every other week to discuss a few chapters of a professional book. These are the kinds of decisions clubs make as they figure out what works for them.

There is, of course, some serious responsibility that comes with students' deciding when and how often they'll meet with their book clubs. You might find that giving students this level of autonomy and choice requires a great deal of flexibility on your part—it's not for the faint of heart. Your classroom might look more like a university library than a traditional classroom, with some individuals reading to themselves while small groups meet and disperse as they see fit. In the midst of these flexible meetings, you'll still need to meet with clubs to assess their progress, help them set new goals, and teach and coach as they approximate new work.

With this model, I've found that I need to be much more comfortable with "on the fly" teaching. Since the students are meeting at various frequencies and for various lengths of time, I need to be more comfortable pulling a chair up next to a club, listening in for a few minutes, and making a decision in the moment about what and how I might teach. In Chapter 4: Utilizing Talk as an Assessment, we'll unpack how you can use the book club's conversation as an assessment that informs responsive teaching.

There is no one right way to schedule book clubs. We know that students need time to read independently, time to jot their ideas and reflections, and time to meet with their book clubs to discuss and develop their

| OPTION A: BOOK CLUBS MEET EVERY DAY | | | | |
|---|---|---|---|---|
| **Monday** | **Tuesday** | **Wednesday** | **Thursday** | **Friday** |
| Independent Reading | Independent Reading | Independent Reading | Independent Reading | Independent Reading |
| Students Meet in Book Clubs | Students Meet in Book Clubs | Students Meet in Book Clubs | Students Meet in Book Clubs | Students Meet in Book Clubs |

| OPTION B: BOOK CLUBS MEET EVERY OTHER DAY | | | | |
|---|---|---|---|---|
| **Monday** | **Tuesday** | **Wednesday** | **Thursday** | **Friday** |
| Independent Reading | Extended Independent Reading | Independent Reading | Extended Independent Reading | Independent Reading |
| Students Meet in Book Clubs | | Students Meet in Book Clubs | | Students Meet in Book Clubs |

| OPTION C: BOOK CLUBS ALTERNATE MEETING DAYS | | | | |
|---|---|---|---|---|
| **Monday** | **Tuesday** | **Wednesday** | **Thursday** | **Friday** |
| Independent Reading | Independent Reading | Independent Reading | Independent Reading | Extended Independent Reading |
| Book Clubs A, B, C meet | Book Clubs D, E, F meet | Book Clubs A, B, C meet | Book Clubs D, E, F meet | |

Figure 3.2: Options for Scheduling Book Clubs

ideas. The goal is to create a predictable schedule that provides time for students to engage with texts in authentic ways. Figure 3.2 scopes out three options for scheduling book clubs' time together.

Meeting the needs of all our students can feel daunting. It is vital to have a clear set of intentions for each day's workshop, or we can end up returning to the neediest book clubs each day, neglecting the book clubs that appear to be running more smoothly, or outright ignoring the needs of readers who are tackling sophisticated texts seemingly with ease. All of our students deserve to be seen by a teacher, to set long-term goals, to learn strategies that help them work toward those goals, and to receive in-the-moment feedback.

Timely and frequent conferences with book clubs are important for another reason. Book clubs provide an opportunity for you to assess students' comprehension and talk skills and to teach in ways that are informed by those assessments. Creating a schedule for yourself, like the one in Figure 3.3, can help you manage the time you have and realistically plan what you want to accomplish each day, week, and unit of study.

**Figure 3.3: Teacher's Schedule**

| Monday | Tuesday | Wednesday | Thursday | Friday |
|--------|---------|-----------|----------|--------|
| Club A | Club B | Club D | Club E | Club A |
| Club C | Confer 1:1 | Confer 1:1 | Confer 1:1 | Confer 1:1 |
| Club E | Club C | Club A | Club B | Club D |

## Club Identity

Years ago, when I was a staff developer at the Teachers College Reading and Writing Project, we noticed that, after launching book clubs, students were showing very few signs of the uptick in engagement we hoped to see. Despite the exciting opportunity to meet with their classmates and discuss books of their choosing, it just felt like a continuation of guided reading groups. During one of our Thursday think-tank meetings, Lucy Calkins announced, "Clubs should be more . . .clubby." She invoked images of other clubs students loved being a part of—the drama club, the tae kwon do club, the running club. These clubs, she said, had strong identities and worked to make their members feel a part of something bigger. We started wondering how we could help our book club members feel this same sense of identity and belonging.

It reminded me of my own adult book club, which I formed with a few friends the year after we graduated from college. Having just finished reading Anita Diamant's *The Red Tent*, we called ourselves The Red Tent Collective. We decided to each invite one other member, to make a group of six. We scheduled a monthly meeting, made a list of books we had been wanting to read, and selected our first book. We decided to rotate our meetings among our tiny Brooklyn apartments and to allow two hours to discuss a book and leave some time to snack and chat. We also decided that each meeting should start with a quick check-in on each other's lives, which we called "Good Thing/Bad Thing." Essentially, we were figuring out how to make ourselves more "clubby"—to foster our group identity, create some rituals, and establish routines that would keep us on track. Couldn't kids do the same?

When you first form clubs, you might invite the groups to select a club name, establish some club norms or commitments, and choose a "clubhouse"—a consistent spot somewhere in the room where they'll meet. As students learn the possible ways clubs can interact and discuss texts, you could even teach them to create a club agenda, much like the agendas we use to keep our team meetings on track. Book clubs might spend time selecting a discussion-worthy idea, rereading sections of the book, reflecting on their goals, and deciding how much to read before they meet again. Mrs. Indelicato, a fifth-grade teacher, even gave her book clubs an opportunity to create a coat of arms (see Figure 3.4).

All of these agreements help to develop a specific identity within the book club. Clubs—whether they focus on books or wine or parenting an infant—develop ways of being together. There are unique ways that club members talk with each other, make plans for what they'll do, decide how

**Figure 3.4**

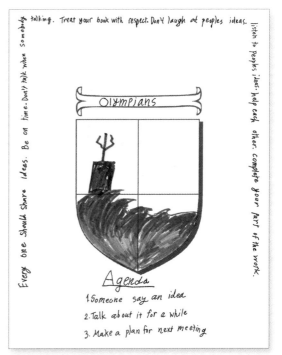

often they'll get together. Making these "clubby" behaviors explicit to students increases the likelihood that they'll continue without us, knowing how to start and sustain their own book clubs. It also sets the groundwork necessary for the challenging task ahead—teaching clubs how to think and talk together to grow increasingly complex ideas.

This kind of work mimics the community building you probably do with your entire class in September—helping them get to know each other, establishing some norms for working and learning together, developing a sense of safety within the group. This is the same type of preliminary identity work students do when they form clubs. In the next chapter, we'll look at more complex identity work clubs engage in, such as setting a clear goal, developing a repertoire of strategic actions, and reflecting on the growth that really transforms a group of students into a Book Club.

## Teaching TIP

Members of a book club need to decide what materials they'll bring each time. In some classrooms, students have reader's notebooks where they jot their thinking. Some book clubs keep a mini anchor chart in a file folder to remind themselves what they're working on.

# CHAPTER 4

# Utilizing Talk as an Assessment

ONE JANUARY, during a particularly dreary and snowy winter, I decided to read the first Harry Potter book with my third-grade class. During opportunities to turn and talk, while others were chatting away about their thoughts, feelings, and predictions, Ciara would sit quietly, listening to her partner gab on and on. Many times, I would scoot close to her and simply ask, "What are you thinking?" I would usually get nothing but a shrug. It was hard to know not just what she was getting but whether she was getting anything at all. Each day, for the first few days, I wondered if I had made a mistake even starting the series.

Then one day, while walking to recess, the dam of Ciara's internal experience broke open. "How can Dudley be so mean to Harry when Harry is so powerful? He's going to regret that he ever treated him this way! And nobody really appreciates him except for Hermione and Ron. And I'm worried about Malfoy! And Voldemort!" Throughout recess I could barely get a word in as she talked on and on about the plot, the characters, their relationships with each other, and how they were each handling their own and each other's struggles. "Oh," I thought. "So *that's* what she's been thinking."

One of the challenges I've found in teaching reading well is that the really important work, the work of making meaning and understanding texts at deep, complex levels, takes place in the mind of each reader. With writing, so much of this type of work can be found on the page, in students' writer's notebooks, or in their drafts. But with reading, we really need some way to get into each student's mind to figure out what they're thinking. Without this information, we might make dangerous assumptions about what they're getting or not getting, thinking or not thinking about the text.

So how do we incorporate an assessment that gives us a fuller picture of the invisible work of reading? How do we truly know what a student is thinking independently? Cris Tovani, a teacher and literacy consultant, once said in a workshop that I attended, "You have to metaphorically open the head and see what the reader is doing. The only way to do that is to get the student to talk about his thinking or to write about his thinking." A student-led discussion in a book club setting provides a perfect opportunity for a teacher to sit back, listen, and assess students' independent thinking. Because the conversation is initiated and led by students, it's an authentic assessment of the work they can do independently. Observing and listening to students' conversations can become another tool to add to our toolbox for a more comprehensive assessment.

## Observing and Listening as Data Collection

If the word "data" conjures up in your mind images of spreadsheets, sorting tools, and labeling students in tiers, you're not alone. To some people, it seems, data have value only if they're quantifiable and measurable. And while numerical data have their purpose, I want us to reimagine data as any information we can gain about what the readers in our class can do or are trying to do. When they pull their hood over their head and put their head down on their desk, that's data. When they ignore our signal to line up for lunch because they're so immersed in the world of their novel, that's data. When they interrupt our read-aloud to share an epiphany they just had about the character's motives, that's data too. This kind of data collection requires that we watch learners closely, listen to what they say, and constantly ask ourselves, "What might this tell me about this reader?"

Noticing students' behavior with you, with their book, and with their book club is a form of data collection because you can use your observations to inform your teaching. Listening to a book club conversation is also a form of data collection because you can use what you hear as a window into the readers' comprehension of a text. The challenge is to get out of the way enough to see what students are capable of on their own. If we consistently launch the conversation with a question, insert ourselves into the conversation to clarify, or prompt students to respond in a certain way, we can no longer see what students are doing because we are heavily guiding them. However, if we set them up and then step out of the way, we can use an authentic book club conversation as a formative assessment for future teaching.

The lightest scaffold you can possibly provide is space and opportunity for a book club conversation. When I'm assessing, I often say something like this: "Today I'm just going to listen in on your book club conversation. Who can get the conversation started today?" If students have experiences with whole-class conversations like the one described in Chapter 2, this prompt will be familiar to them, and they'll likely be able to launch a book club conversation.

You might be wondering, "What if students don't talk to each other at all?" That's data! If nobody in the book club is able to provide an idea or a question that launches the book club into a discussion, that provides you with some information about your first teaching steps. They need to be taught *how* readers start a conversation or *how* readers mine their reader's notebooks for ideas to bring to their book club. Or they might even need to be taught *how* readers develop discussion-worthy ideas as they read.

Another option is to make note of the need for future teaching and then help the students get the conversation going. This slightly heavier scaffold might start with something like this: "Who has an idea or a question about the characters that could get the conversation started?" An even heavier scaffold could be something like this: "I was thinking about how the character Moth is discovering her own history and how that's changing how she feels about herself. What do you think about that?" These scaffolds are ways to get the conversation going so that you can listen more and collect more data. But it's important to take note of your role, because it reveals that initiating a conversation isn't quite under the students' control yet and that you'll need to teach, coach, and reinforce the behavior over time.

Remember, the goal is to assess what students can do independently. So both your words and your actions need to communicate to them that they're the ones running the show. In a fourth-grade classroom, I once watched a student ask the teacher to physically back away from the book club so the members could more easily talk to each other. Decentering yourself physically can have a powerful effect in shifting the sense of responsibility to the students.

## Analyzing the Assessment

Once students are talking, the real test of a teacher's willpower begins. In their conversations, we hear confusions about the text. We hear students who fall back on retelling, jumping from scene to scene, sometimes in no particular order. We hear students going around the circle sharing idea after idea seemingly without listening or responding to each other. It is difficult in these moments to resist the urge to jump in and teach. We want to clarify a student's misconception about the setting. We want to push the student to respond to the idea that was just shared rather than moving on to a new, unrelated idea. And we want to coach students beyond the plot into more inferential and interpretive thinking. We want to fix the glaring problems we see.

Instead of teaching right away, consider taking a transcript and leaving yourself a minute or two to analyze it in order to make a clearer, more informed decision. When you're first using student talk as a formal assessment, it's difficult to both listen and determine what kinds of comprehension and conversation skills readers are using. Conversations often move quickly, and by the time you've mentally processed the first student's comment, the fourth or fifth student is talking. So, in the beginning stages, I suggest taking a transcript as a *temporary* scaffold until you can notice and name, on the fly, the work students are doing. Once you've trained yourself to listen in this way, a full transcript becomes less necessary. Still, I've found that in the beginning it's a useful tool. For our purposes, throughout this book I include verbatim transcripts I've taken of book club discussions. But as you can see in Figure 4.1, my actual transcripts are far less polished. In reality, I try to get the gist of what students are saying so that I can analyze their strengths and next steps at a later time.

There are many ways to analyze student talk, but this book will focus on analyzing it through two lenses: conversation skills and comprehension skills. First, we analyze the transcript for what it tells us about *how students talk* to each other. What does this transcript show us about the students' conversations skills? And next, we return to the same transcript with a different lens: What does it tell us about *their understanding of the text*, or comprehension? In this way, we can support students in how they *think* about texts and also in how they *talk* about texts. First, we'll take a close look at conversation skills.

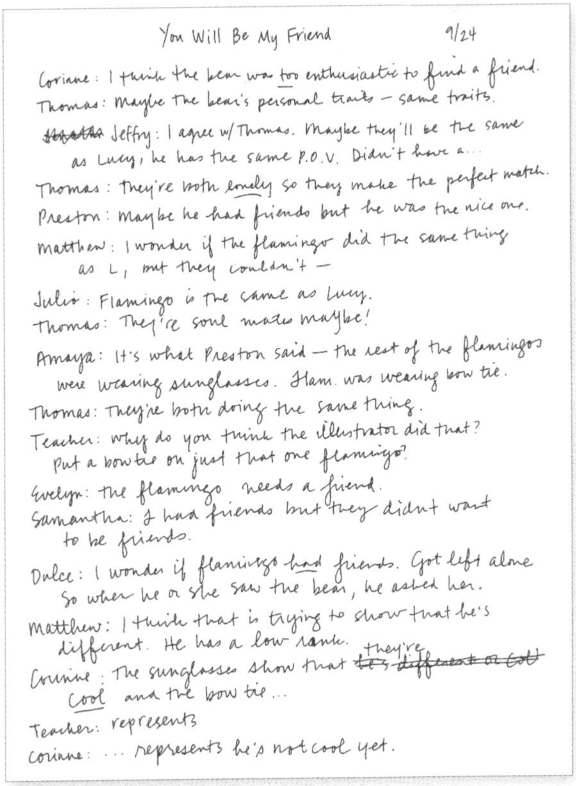
You Will Be My Friend 9/24

Corinne: I think the bear was too enthusiastic to find a friend.
Thomas: Maybe the bear's personal traits — same traits.
Jeffry: I agree w/ Thomas. Maybe they'll be the same as Lucy, he has the same P.O.V. Didn't have a...
Thomas: They're both lonely so they make the perfect match.
Preston: Maybe he had friends but he was the nice one.
Matthew: I wonder if the flamingo did the same thing as L, but they couldn't —
Julio: Flamingo is the same as Lucy.
Thomas: They're soul mates maybe!
Amaya: It's what Preston said — the rest of the flamingos were wearing sunglasses. Flam. was wearing bow tie.
Thomas: They're both doing the same thing.
Teacher: Why do you think the illustrator did that? Put a bow tie on just that one flamingo?
Evelyn: The flamingo needs a friend.
Samantha: I had friends but they didn't want to be friends.
Dulce: I wonder if flamingos had friends. Got left alone so when he or she saw the bear, he asked her.
Matthew: I think that is trying to show that he's different. He has a low rank.
Corinne: The sunglasses show that ~~he's different or cool~~ they're cool and the bow tie...
Teacher: represents
Corinne: ... represents he's not cool yet.

**Figure 4.1**

Handwritten transcripts don't have to be perfect, as long as they help you analyze student conversation and think about where to go next.

## Conversation

Lunch bunch has always been one of my favorite times as a classroom teacher. Hosting a small group of kids in the classroom when the rest of the group is in the cafeteria feels awkward but exciting at the same time and gives us a window into whole new worlds of the kids in our class. Entire lunch periods can fly by without any participation on my end as kids yap and yammer about their favorite toys, a birthday party at Chuck E. Cheese, or a teacher they had the year before. One teacher I know calls this unstructured social time "networking." Kids know how to talk to each other when the expectations of academic talk are removed.

During these times, I started paying close attention to these student-centered conversations. What were children doing that helped them sustain that conversation? What were the actual moves these conversationalists used naturally that I could help them transfer to an academic context?

They were asking each other questions. They agreed and added on and challenged each other's thinking. They gave other examples from their lives. They shared their opinions and reactions. They also sat in silence while they thought of what to say next and seemed perfectly comfortable with that too.

A productive conversation is an incredibly powerful comprehension tool. The process of sharing our ideas with someone, listening intently to others' thoughts, and revising our own thinking helps us respond to texts and also to the world around us. A conversation is not merely a way to tell someone what you think, although that might be a starting place for some students. Powerful conversations are the vehicles through which ideas are developed. It is through discussion with others that ideas are tested, changed, and made more complex.

Although group discussions can be chaotic and messy, there are patterns, or types of talk people use when engaging in an academic conversation. By analyzing student conversations, we can identify skills students show control over, skills they are attempting, and skills that have not yet developed. We can then reinforce their strengths and teach them to have increasingly sophisticated academic conversations.

While different researchers have created their own categories for various types of conversation skills, I rely heavily on the work of Zwiers and Crawford (2011), as presented in their book *Academic Conversations*, which emphasizes the following core conversation skills:

## Academic Conversation Skills

| SKILL | HOW IT MIGHT SOUND IN PRACTICE |
|---|---|
| **Elaborating and Clarifying** | I think . . .<br>This might mean . . .<br>One idea I had was . . .<br>This is important because . . . |
| **Supporting with Examples** | For example . . .<br>That's like on page . . .<br>In the book it says . . . |

| SKILL | HOW IT MIGHT SOUND IN PRACTICE |
|---|---|
| **Building On and/or Challenging a Partner's Idea** | Yes, and . . . <br> To build on to your idea . . . <br> On the other hand . . . <br> Or maybe . . . |
| **Paraphrasing** | So, you're saying . . . <br> In other words . . . <br> So, you think . . . |
| **Summarizing Discussion Points** | So, the big ideas seem to be . . . <br> So, we think . . . and also . . . |

These conversation skills are helpful because they give us clear categories to analyze students' discussions about books based on authentic academic conversations. Let's use these five conversation skills to look at a transcript and analyze what conversational strengths the students already have and what we might need to teach them. This club of third-grade students has just read the first half of the picture book *Fox* by Margaret Wild and Ron Brooks.

**Cesar:** Maybe Magpie went on Fox because Fox is more faster and Dog is slower. Magpie went on Fox to make sure he is faster than Dog or he's like trying to trick her.

**Cooper:** Magpie shouldn't go because Dog was going fast. The story even *says* it—that she had to "hold on tight." It's going to get out of control.

**Leylani:** Fox is tricking her to break her other wing. She'll be nothing without wings.

**Teresa:** I agree. If she breaks her other wing, she'll be nothing. But I also think Fox is trying to replace Dog and be Magpie's friend. He was lonely before. Because he could have just asked if he could be both of their friends.

**Book Club:**
Star Readers

**Title of Book:**
*Fox*

**Leylani:** I kind of disagree. Fox isn't going to break her wing. He'll let her fall off and let it break on its own.

**Brianna:** I think you could go back to that page with Fox's eyes. Why anger? We know loneliness. But why anger? I think Fox has lost a friend before, he's taking it out on Magpie and Dog.

**Teresa:** I agree with Leylani. He's trying to make her break her own wing. Magpie went with Fox because he could run faster.

**Brianna:** Maybe Fox lost a friend. He's releasing the anger on them. It'll make him feel better to take it out on Magpie.

Whenever we look at assessments, Marie Clay (2016) reminds us in *Literacy Lessons*, it is most helpful to approach them with a strengths model rather than a deficit model. In a deficit model, our eyes are tuned into what students aren't doing. We look for errors or omissions or what there is no evidence of, and these observations inform our instruction. On the other hand, in a strengths model, our lens is the opposite. Clay suggests that we put aside our assumptions about students and instead "listen very carefully and record very precisely what that particular child can in fact do" (2016, 12). We ask, "What are students controlling or partially controlling?" It turns out these questions lead us to the kind of instruction that lands squarely in the students' zone of proximal development (ZPD). In the ZPD, students can successfully learn new behaviors and skills *with the support of* a more proficient adult or peer. If students are showing evidence of approximating, or trying something, we can teach them to do it better, to control it more. For that reason, we start by looking at the transcript for what students are attempting or partially controlling.

These third-grade students are about two weeks into their first book club unit. This is only the seventh time they've met as a group to have a conversation. And while the conversation isn't always linear, we can see evidence of a few important skills. Cesar and Brianna are showing evidence that they can **put a discussion-worthy idea on the table**. ("Maybe Magpie went on Fox because . . . ," "But why anger? I think Fox has lost a friend before . . .")

Once the students have an idea on the table, they start to support that idea with examples from the text. ("The story even says it—that she had to 'hold on tight,'" "I think you could go back to that page with Fox's eyes.") With each example, the club is **supporting the idea** that Cesar or Brianna put forward—that Fox is trying to trick her and that he's angry.

There's also evidence of **building on or challenging an idea**. Some students build on the idea that Fox is tricking Magpie ("It's going to get out of control," "Fox is tricking her to break her other wing") and later challenge the idea by suggesting other options ("I kind of disagree. He'll let her fall off and let it break on its own.").

After noting what students are controlling or approximating, we turn our attention to what might be some next steps for this group in terms of conversation skills. Once again, we remember to focus on strengths rather than jumping immediately to what students are not attempting. The most powerful teaching and learning take place when we start from what the students are partially controlling. Marie Clay (2016) reminds us that we help students learn by connecting what is known to what is new. In this case, we could choose a conversation skill that one or two of the students in the book club are using and teach the rest of the members to try it. In this conversation, Cesar puts forth a discussion-worthy idea and the others then support his idea with examples from the text. One thing we might teach this group is how *other* members could **start a discussion with their own idea** the way Cesar did. In this case, Cesar serves as the model for the rest of the group to try something new.

Another possible next step might be to teach the group to **support ideas with examples**. While Cooper gave specific evidence from the text for why he felt it was going to get "out of control," we could teach other students to support their thinking in the same way. Students expressed multiple explanations for Fox's behavior: he's tricking Magpie, he's lonely and wants to be her friend, he's angry and is taking it out on her. It would be useful for them to cite specific parts of the text to support their theories.

Here's an example of what my notes look like after listening to this group.

**Analysis of Conversation Skills for a Third-Grade Book Club**

|  | CONVERSATION | COMPREHENSION |
|---|---|---|
| **Noticed** | • Putting an idea on the table (Cesar, Brianna)<br>• Building on/challenging (Cooper, Teresa, Leylani)<br>• Supporting ideas with examples (Cooper, Brianna) | |
| **Next Steps** | • Putting an idea on the table (expand to the whole group)<br>• Supporting ideas with examples (expand to the whole group) | |

## Comprehension

Analyzing conversation skills is an important step in determining what students know about *how* to engage in academic discourse about texts. Student conversations also provide us with essential information about the kinds of thinking students are doing and the meaning they are making about the texts as they read. In order to determine these things, we need to listen with a completely different focus—that of comprehension.

In the case of comprehension, there isn't a single list of skills or strategies. Depending on which professional texts we consult, the lists have slight variations. Fountas and Pinnell (2017a) organize their strategic actions into categories of "beyond the text" and "about the text." Calkins (2015) and others at the Reading and Writing Project break theirs into strands with subcategories that progress in sophistication. It is difficult for comprehension skills to be separated into neat categories because we know they are interconnected and dependent on one another.

## Comprehension Skills

| SKILL | HOW IT MIGHT SOUND IN PRACTICE |
|---|---|
| **Activating Prior Knowledge** | This reminds me of that other book . . .<br>So that makes me think . . . |
| **Analyzing** | I noticed the author is . . .<br>This book is organized . . . |
| **Critiquing** | The author believes that . . . , but I think . . .<br>The author perpetuates the belief that . . . |
| **Determining Importance** | The important part here is . . . |
| **Inferring About Characters/Topics** | I think the character . . .<br>One thought I had about the character was . . . |
| **Interpreting** | This might represent . . .<br>I think the author is trying to say . . . |
| **Predicting** | I think she might . . . because . . . |
| **Synthesizing** | This part is important because earlier in the book . . .<br>This scene connects to the other scene when . . . |
| **Questioning** | I wonder why/how/what . . . |
| **Visualizing** | I'm imagining . . . |

In *What Readers Really Do*, Dorothy Barnhouse and Vicky Vinton (2012) remind us that the outcome of our instruction is not the *kind* of thinking or the strategy students employ; the outcome is not the strategic action or the skill. These are merely the tools readers use to get to the good stuff: the meaning and ideas. Skills and strategies are the cognitive tools readers use to construct that meaning and develop those ideas. Thus, looking at the *kinds* of thinking readers do is a step toward our ultimate outcome, because it provides us with lenses to analyze the meaning-making going on in book club conversations. After we teach visualizing, for example, a reader's conversation may sound like this: "I visualized Fox running. He was running fast and Magpie was on his back and the wind was blowing his hair." In this case, we have evidence that the student is indeed visualizing. What we don't have is evidence that they are *using* their visualization to make meaning and develop ideas about the text. Any skills and strategies need to be in service of constructing the larger, deeper meaning. But if, instead, the skills and strategies become the endgame, then they are actually getting in the way of readers doing their most important work.

With all of that said, however, it can be helpful, especially when readers struggle, to offer explicit instruction around skills and strategic actions that support readers in constructing meaning. For this reason, we analyze their talk for the kinds of thinking they are already doing. And once again, we turn to a strengths model to determine what strategies students are already using and approximating.

First, we consider student dialogue and ask ourselves questions such as "What is the reader doing?" or "What kinds of thinking is this reader engaging in?" It might be helpful to consult a list of comprehension skills as a starting point, but rather than answering these questions with a single word from the list (e.g., "summarizing"), we try to describe the student's talk with a phrase that elaborates on the skill (e.g., "summarizing major event from each chapter" or "summarizing interactions between main and secondary characters"). Let's try this with a couple of excerpts from the transcript we looked at earlier.

## Analyzing Student Talk

| What is the student saying? | What is the reader doing to understand the text? |
|---|---|
| "Maybe Magpie went on Fox because Fox is more faster and Dog is slower. Magpie went on Fox to make sure he is faster than Dog or he's like trying to trick her." | Inferring about a character's explicit or hidden motivations |
| "I think you could go back to that page with Fox's eyes. Why anger? We know loneliness. But why anger?" | Questioning the cause of a character's emotions and actions |
| "Fox is tricking her to break her other wing. She'll be nothing without wings." | Predicting a character's actions and the impact on other characters |

After listening to this conversation, my notes for the group looked like this:

## Analysis of Comprehension Skills for a Third-Grade Book Club

| | CONVERSATION | COMPREHENSION |
|---|---|---|
| **Noticed** | • Putting an idea on the table (Cesar, Brianna)<br>• Building on/challenging (Cooper, Teresa, Leylani)<br>• Supporting ideas with examples (Cooper, Brianna) | • Inferring about a character's explicit or hidden motivations<br>• Questioning the cause of a character's emotions and actions<br>• Predicting a character's actions and the impact on other characters |
| **Next Steps** | • Putting an idea on the table (expand to the whole group)<br>• Supporting ideas with examples (expand to the whole group) | |

Once we've determined what students are already doing, we can think about how to build on their strengths and approximations. These students already know that it's useful and important to start building an idea about the characters. Most of their conversation focuses on understanding Fox's motivation and exploring the possibilities. One possible next step for this group would be to develop a more complex theory that involves analysis of multiple sides of a character and conflicting motivations. For example, exploring the idea that Fox might be cruel and angry while also being lonely and in need of friendship might lead to some rich conversation.

Another area to develop is the difference between what characters overtly communicate about themselves and what is implicitly communicated. Analyzing how characters might say one thing but feel or do another helps us see them as nuanced rather than one-dimensional. It helps students develop a sense that characters, like people, are complex and multifaceted. Both of these options are included in the completed chart.

## Complete Analysis of a Third-Grade Book Club

|  | CONVERSATION | COMPREHENSION |
|---|---|---|
| **Noticed** | • Putting an idea on the table (Cesar, Brianna)<br><br>• Building on/challenging (Cooper, Teresa, Leylani)<br><br>• Supporting ideas with examples (Cooper, Brianna) | • Inferring about a character's explicit or hidden motivations<br><br>• Questioning the cause of a character's emotions and actions<br><br>• Predicting a character's actions and the impact on other characters |
| **Next Steps** | • Putting an idea on the table (expand to the whole group)<br><br>• Supporting ideas with examples (expand to the whole group) | • Developing complex, multifaceted theories about characters<br><br>• Analyzing explicit versus implicit feelings, thoughts, and motivations |

We can use this same type of analysis during a discussion in a non-fiction book club. The transcript that follows details a conversation from a sixth-grade book club in the midst of a nonfiction unit. The group stopped in the middle of reading *Separate Is Never Equal* to discuss their ideas so far.

**Book Club:**
Best Book Club

**Title of Book:**
*Separate Is Never Equal*

**Teacher:** Can someone get us started?

**Josue:** I'm noticing how they're describing—I don't know how to say her name. Sylvia? They're describing her brothers and her—let's say, how she talks, her beliefs, how she looks. And I think it doesn't matter how you look or how you sound or how you look like. You should always be treated the same—equally.

**Douglas:** I agree with Josue. Since everyone has different personalities, but they're also the same and we're supposed to respect everyone the same. It's not like one race is better than the other.

**All:** Yeah, yeah.

[pause]

**Josue:** They're really getting a lot of discrimination. They have to go, like, to this school: (Reading) "In the city of Westminster." How they can't attend a better school than this just, not good school.

**Tatiana:** I thought, I was thinking, on page (flipping through the book), these four pages, where they get enrolled, I noticed the secretary was being, like, mean to them by not giving them an enrollment form. She didn't even say anything. They asked for an enrollment form for all of them and then she only gave her two and then she was like, "I can't do that for the people."

**Josue:** Yeah, it said the secretary said, "They must go to the Mexican school." Over here on the first page it says, "She was looking for her locker when a young white boy pointed at her and yelled, 'Go back to the Mexico school! You don't belong here.'" So they're discriminating her a lot. They're discriminating everything.

**Douglas:** Yeah, just because of her skin color.

**Josue:** And their last names too!

**Tatiana:** I noticed that they keep saying, "Go back to the Mexican school", in the very, very, very beginning the kid said, "Go back to the Mexican school. You don't belong here." And then on page 8, the secretary said, "They must go to the Mexican school."

**Teacher:** So, it seems like one of the big issues, the deeper messages, you all have been talking about is this idea of injustice or discrimination.

**Douglas:** Racism!

**Teacher:** Racism, right?

**Douglas:** Yeah, because there's a part when they met another family and then they said that that guy worked on . . . went to World War II and helped. And then the author's trying to say that even when they make impacts in this country, they . . . still don't let them get freedom.

This club was able to bring a lot of what they knew from their work in a previous fiction unit into this nonfiction unit because they were reading narrative nonfiction texts. Josue starts off right away sharing an idea ("I'm noticing . . ." and "I think . . ."). and Douglas **builds on** to the initial idea ("I agree . . . It's not like one race is better than the other"). Tatiana **supports** an idea **with an example**, taking her club to specific pages and lines of the book ("on these four pages . . ."), and immediately Josue does the same ("Yeah, it said the secretary said . . ."). During the rest of the conversation, students find specific examples from the text to support the larger idea (a community facing discrimination) originally put on the table.

These students are skilled at building on someone else's idea by supporting it. The teacher steps in at the end of the conversation to **paraphrase** the club's thinking. This is a very useful skill that allows all members to feel heard so they can move on to another, new idea once the current one is exhausted. Learning to paraphrase each other without teacher support would be a useful next step for the club members.

The book club was also quick to build consensus, sign off on Josue's original idea, and support it. While this was useful to a point, we might teach the skill of **challenging an idea** as a way to complicate their thinking. For example, while the students focused solely on the injustice of the discrimination, a book club member might have challenged or complicated the idea by saying, "On the other hand, they had lots of ways of fighting against the discrimination; they weren't just victims."

Next, we analyze this same conversation for what it reveals about the students' comprehension. Josue starts the conversation by **interpreting** the larger social issues and themes in the text—how people are discriminated against based on their physical appearance and language. Together, Josue, Tatiana, and Douglas gather multiple examples to **identify a pattern** in the narrative—the ways in which the character's family faced discrimination. Tatiana takes it further, to **infer** the meaning of the actions of one of the characters, the secretary.

Based on their current comprehension, we might develop some possible next steps for the group to deepen their understanding and discussion. Whenever a group is analyzing a single topic, character, or theme, one option we have is to help them explore that element from multiple angles. So we could teach the club to **explore multiple themes** and messages.

While this group is noticing one of the larger themes, they aren't noticing or discussing the tiny details the author and illustrator have included to develop those themes. So another option would be to teach them how to mine symbolic details, such as reoccurring objects, images, and words, and **interpret** their deeper meaning.

Since this group is so focused on social issues and so aware of the social messages the author is communicating, we might also help them develop a **critical lens**, analyzing whose perspective or voice is centered in the text and whose is marginalized or silenced.

Here are my notes based on my analysis of this club's conversation.

### Complete Analysis of a Sixth-Grade Book Club

| | CONVERSATION | COMPREHENSION |
|---|---|---|
| **Noticed** | • Building on<br>• Supporting idea with examples | • Interpreting theme/message<br>• Synthesizing multiple parts, identifying a pattern<br>• Inferring about character actions, motivations |
| **Next Steps** | • Paraphrasing<br>• Challenging (or complicating) ideas | • Exploring other possible themes and messages (not just a single one)<br>• Interpreting symbolic actions, objects, etc.<br>• Critiquing author's perspective, whose voice is included, who is privileged in the text |

It's important to note that there is no "one correct next step." There are multiple next steps these students are ready for, and selecting *one* to teach is more powerful than mentioning many and moving quickly through a list of teaching points. The process of listening to students talk, taking a transcript, and analyzing that transcript for strengths and next steps provides us with a menu of options for our teaching. In fact, analyzing this one transcript provides us with enough information to sustain our work with this group for a couple of weeks. Rather than rushing to cover all the possibilities, we want to select a high-leverage next step and teach well, returning to assess the group's control over it across texts and genres. In Chapter 5, we'll look at possible ways to teach and to check on the effectiveness of our teaching.

## Reasons to Take a Transcript

As mentioned earlier, taking a transcript is a (temporary) scaffold you might put in place for yourself as you learn to assess using students' talk. Some teachers are so adept  at listening for conversation and comprehension skills that, rather than taking a transcript to analyze later, they go directly to the Noticed/Next Steps Matrix, presented in this chapter and in Appendix A, jotting down strengths and next steps as students are in the midst of discussing their book. Ultimately, you might decide you need to take a transcript when you want to accomplish any of these goals:

- collect some "baseline data" to inform future instruction
- see what students are taking on independently from your teaching
- give yourself some time to reflect and analyze students' conversations more closely

## Redefining "Assessment"

Traditionally, the word "assessment" has conjured up images of students sitting at desks, with file folders propped up for privacy or to prevent cheating. The purpose of an assessment was to test students. The question was "Did they get it?" In more traditional models, instruction stopped when there was an assessment. "I'm not teaching today," a teacher might say. "I'm giving an assessment." Assessment was something that interrupted the ongoing work that happened regularly in our classrooms. The problem with this form of assessment is described by Irene Fountas and Gay Su Pinnell in *Guided Reading*, Second Edition: "If assessment is considered to be 'separate' from instruction, it will always be superfluous, ineffective, even a dreaded and annoying interruption. Yet without effective assessment, instruction will be merely guesswork" (2017b, 214).

The question, then, is how we can use what students are already doing—reading, writing, thinking, and talking—as the assessment. If there are constant opportunities for students to talk to each other, share their current understanding, and construct new understandings together, then an authentic formative assessment is already built into our day. There is no need to stop instruction, to stop reading, to stop discussion in order to assess. Students' daily habits of thinking about their books and discussing their thinking are always available to us if we listen carefully. We're always wondering, "What are students controlling and what might be some next steps?" We can only start to know the answers to these questions if we step back and allow students to show us, even through their approximations, what they control.

# CHAPTER 5

# Teaching for Comprehension and Conversation

YOU MIGHT REMEMBER from earlier chapters that cooking is not my forte and that it usually takes me weeks of internal pep talks to plan and make a simple dinner for four. A while back, as my husband sampled my latest attempt at soup, he asked innocently, "Did you taste this soup?" I'm not kidding when I say it had literally never occurred to me to taste the soup before serving it. I followed the recipe, completed each step, used all the ingredients as instructed. If I'm being really honest, I usually don't taste food before I serve it because I don't have a very strong sense of agency when it comes to cooking. In other words, if the food isn't good, I'm probably not going to know how to fix it or make it taste any better. The best I can do is find a reliable recipe and stick to the plan!

Skilled home cooks, on the other hand, taste as they cook because they know that a recipe will lead to different outcomes depending on any number of factors—what kind of oven is being used (fancy restaurant oven versus tiny, old New York City–apartment oven), whether the asparagus is in season, or whether the lemons are fresh off the tree or have been sitting in the fridge for three weeks. Chefs know that even a tried-and-true recipe needs to be tasted and adjusted along the way. If they follow the recipe and the food isn't seasoned enough, chefs don't shrug (as I usually do) and say, "Well, that's what the recipe said to do." They probably add some salt and pepper and taste it again.

While I haven't (yet) developed these instincts in the kitchen, over the years, I've had to develop these instincts in the classroom. Skilled teachers, like skilled chefs, know that the magic is found not only in a well-planned lesson (or recipe), although that's a helpful and essential starting place. Teachers know that we plan our language, consider our teaching moves, select texts we think will inspire, *and* we notice and respond to what students give us in the moment.

In this chapter, I lay out first the ways we plan to teach book clubs purposefully and deliberately and then the ways we inevitably tweak our plans and respond flexibly to the readers in front of us, who will surprise us each day.

## Prioritizing

In my second year of teaching, I was lucky enough to work with Kathleen Tolan at the Teachers College Reading and Writing Project in New York City. While we were reflecting together on conferring, she made this observation: "Sometimes in our lessons, we mention a lot. And when we *mention* a lot, we don't *teach* anything." She let that sink in for a moment. What, I wondered, was the difference between *mentioning* something and *teaching* it? In an effort to address comprehension with a reading group, I sometimes prompted for visualizing, listening to others, following the journey of the main character, supporting an idea with examples, and rereading when there was confusion. And yet, if I analyzed what new work I had actually *taught*—modeled, coached, reinforced, moved into independent practice—I'm not sure that I could name any one thing. In my effort to address all the priorities, I ended up teaching none of them. To avoid the trap of merely mentioning multiple things to a book club, the first step is to determine and commit to a clear focus for teaching.

In order to prioritize, I return to the Noticed/Next Steps Matrix used for assessments in Chapter 3 and reproduced in Appendix A. This four-quadrant chart reminds us that students will need to be taught, coached, and supported in both comprehension (the development of ideas to understand their book) and conversation (the development of academic discourse and communication). If we focus our teaching solely on comprehension, our readers may develop more complex ideas, but they will still be unsure how to use the conversation to build a deeper, socially constructed understanding. For example, in the following book club, the readers in the group discuss *The Secrets of Droon*.

> **Katrina:** I wondered on page fifty-two—why does the air smell like smoke?

> **Shayla:** I'm thinking the person who grabbed her might have stopped because he . . .the king is powerful.

> **Emma:** I wonder why Keeah's dad kept running after them.

> **Solei:** I could really imagine this land and how different it is from their home. I bet it didn't even make sense to them at first.

> **Shayla:** Another thing I'm wondering is how that stone is so powerful.

**Book Club:**
Recess Queens

**Title of Book:**
*The Secrets of Droon*

Notice how the students share their thoughts round-robin style, each student telling the others their idea with little interaction or response. This interaction reminds me of the concept of parallel play we discussed in Chapter 2. Teaching that focuses solely on comprehension can lead to "parallel talk" during book clubs, with each student putting their idea out for the group potentially to ignore.

On the other side of this balance are conversation skills. If we focus our teaching solely on academic conversation, students may respond to each other, support an idea with examples, and disagree, but the content and complexity of the actual idea being discussed might be shallow. Students may "perform" an academic conversation using sentence frames such as "I agree with you because . . ." or "I'd like to add on to your idea," but the idea they are talking about may be simplistic or literal. Take a look at this exchange among students engaged in an academic conversation about the main character in the graphic novel *The Bad Guys*.

**Gustavo:** The wolf really wants to be a good guy, but he can't.

**Edwardo:** Yeah, I agree with you. For example, in the text he says, "How will anyone take us seriously?"

**Gustavo:** I want to add on to that. He wants to be great guys but he says they're . . . [looking in the book] misunderstood?

**Valeria:** Yeah! On the other hand, people don't know he's a good guy.

In this example, though the students are constructing an understanding through talk, the idea (that the wolf wants us to think he's not a bad guy) is more literal and clearly explained through the text.

Comprehension and conversation skills are interdependent. One doesn't trump the other. They both need to be developed simultaneously. Since you might not teach both on the same day, it's important to toggle back and forth throughout a unit so that both are developed and can support each other. As students' ideas become richer, their conversation becomes more sophisticated. As students learn how to talk in more sophisticated ways, the conversation supports more sophisticated idea development. Comprehension and conversation are symbiotic.

# Crafting a Worthy Goal

Selecting a goal or two for a book club based on your assessment is tricky business. Goals are selected, but also tweaked and revised, elevated or simplified based on more information in the form of more assessment. When I'm crafting goals for a club, I tend to ask myself a few guiding questions:

1. **Is it in the students' zone of proximal development (ZPD)?**

   In a deficit model of thinking, we search for something the students are not controlling or doing and use that to set a goal. In a strengths-based model we search for something students are approximating, or trying on with some control, and use *that* to set a goal. If there is evidence of students trying something, even unsuccessfully, it usually means they are ready to learn to be more strategic and might be successful with a teacher's instruction and support.

2. **Is it the right size?**

   I tend to think of a goal as something that can be worked toward across a unit of study, which is usually three to five weeks. I want the goal to be lofty enough that it will take multiple attempts, in different books, across a month or so to see a shift. If the goal is too big, students won't feel successful or might get frustrated or bored with the goal. On the other hand, if the goal is too small, they might show mastery immediately. If I teach something and the book club immediately shows mastery or complete control, it's usually because they knew how to do it in the first place and the goal wasn't challenging enough. Matt Glover and Mary Alice Berry (2012) remind us that our daily teaching will build toward our unit goals.

3. **Are there multiple pathways toward this goal?**

   Without getting too caught up in jargon, I want to clarify the difference between a goal and a strategy. The goal is the larger "what" students are working toward. The goal is something authentic and actionable that readers do, in multiple contexts and across time. A strategy is simply one process, or "how," that helps students build toward that goal. A goal is most attainable for a variety of students if there are multiple pathways, or strategies, that help them work toward it.

In Figure 5.1 you'll find some examples and non-examples of goals for book clubs. Of course, students in a book club can also generate their own goals, but this probably will require that they have some models first.

| NON-EXAMPLES OF GOALS | EXAMPLES OF GOALS |
|---|---|
| Readers use the Somebody-Wanted-But-So graphic organizer to prepare for their book club conversation. [This goal is too heavily scaffolded; it doesn't provide multiple pathways.] | Readers jot their thinking along the way to prepare for their book club conversation. [There are multiple pathways to this goal because there are many ways readers can jot their thinking.] |
| Readers develop theories about Moth in *The Okay Witch* and her relationships with her friends and mom. [This goal is too narrow and text-specific; it doesn't provide opportunities to transfer to other texts and genres.] | Readers develop and revise theories about main and secondary characters and the relationships between them. [This goal can transfer across multiple texts and genres.] |
| Readers look at each other when they speak. [This goal is too low-level; students are probably already approximating and will be frustrated and bored working solely on this.] | Readers build on and challenge each other's ideas to sustain a conversation about a single idea. [This goal is appropriately ambitious—it might take multiple weeks to observe growth.] |

Figure 5.1

With all of these examples in mind, let's look back at the Noticed/Next Steps Matrix from the discussion of *Fox*, which we analyzed in Chapter 4, and use that data to set a worthy goal for the book club.

### Noticed/Next Steps Matrix for a Third-Grade Book Club

| | CONVERSATION | COMPREHENSION |
|---|---|---|
| **Noticed** | • Putting an idea on the table (Cesar, Brianna)<br>• Building on/challenging (Cooper, Teresa, Leylani)<br>• Support ideas with examples (Cooper, Brianna) | • Inferring about a character's explicit or hidden motivations<br>• Questioning the cause of a character's emotions and actions<br>• Predicting a character's actions and the impact on other characters |
| **Next Steps** | • Putting an idea on the table (expand to whole group)<br>• Supporting ideas with examples (expand to whole group) | • Developing complex, multifaceted theories about characters<br>• Analyzing explicit versus implicit feelings, thoughts, and motivations |

Based on my observations and some past transcripts, I narrowed my instructional focus to a couple of next steps for this group—one comprehension goal and one conversation goal. I used the three questions discussed earlier to check that each is a worthy goal.

## Evaluating Goals

| Goal | CONVERSATION | COMPREHENSION |
| --- | --- | --- |
| | Putting an idea on the table | Developing complex, multifaceted theories about characters |
| **Is it within the students' ZPD?** | Based on the transcript, one or two students are showing evidence of starting the conversation with an idea. Other students probably need explicit teaching and heavier scaffolding in order to do this. | I have evidence that a couple of the group members are developing theories, so they could serve as models for the others. In addition, developing *multifaceted* theories is *slightly* more sophisticated than what they are currently doing, which is analyzing character motivation or traits. |
| **Is it the right size?** | I'm not sure if this is a large enough goal for the book club. While I think it's an important goal, my guess is that it would take a week or two to show some mastery. With a couple of strategies, some modeling, and a little bit of coaching, students will probably take this on. I'll need to have another goal on deck for when I see evidence of this. | I imagine that this goal would take a couple of weeks because readers would need to synthesize many parts of a book or novel to see the multiple sides of a character. In addition, I would want to see that they transfer this skill to a few different texts. |
| **Are there multiple pathways toward this goal?** | Since this is a small goal, the book club might need only one or two strategies. I can imagine showing them my own process for coming up with an idea to discuss and inviting Cesar or Brianna to share their process for coming up with an idea. | There are multiple strategies (or ways) to achieve this goal. Some students might be analyzing the main or secondary characters and their internal struggles, while others might be developing theories about the relationships between characters. Still others might be tracking how the main character is gradually changing throughout the text. |

# From Planning to Teaching

Setting priorities and goals for each book club is an essential first step because it will provide you with a clear aim for your teaching for the next couple of weeks. As a young teacher, I used to think that selecting a learning target was the extent of the planning I needed. Now I know better—having a goal in mind is just the first step in planning.

Some might see book clubs as an opportunity for students to engage in academic discourse completely independently. But in my mind, any time students participate in authentic, rigorous literacy tasks, it's an opportunity for us to assess what they know (which I've discussed in previous chapters), *and* it's an opportunity for us to teach them. In the following sections, we'll explore instructional opportunities and predictable structures to teach comprehension and conversation.

## Teaching for Comprehension in Book Clubs

When I confer individually with members of a book club, I often start by asking, "What are you thinking so far? What ideas do you have?" Sometimes, these questions are all the prompting kids need to share their thinking and elaborate with examples across the text. These questions work if the readers are already in the habit of forming ideas and carrying them across texts to develop more complex theories. However, there are also readers who aren't in the habit of doing this, so these same questions can leave them feeling as if they had been caught in the act or had missed the assignment. They might stare at me sheepishly or shrug and say, "I don't know." If that's the case, I know I can't wait until they've already read the book and then ask them to develop ideas. Instead, I need to set them up in a way that supports idea development, and then I need to coach them, while they're in the midst of reading, to continue this habit.

### Before Reading: Launching Book Clubs with New Texts

You probably have lot of background knowledge and experience crafting book introductions that support readers with the first read of a text during interactive read-aloud and guided reading. You might already know how to summarize major plot points, "debug the book" by explaining challenging text and language structures, and even highlight essential new vocabulary students will need to understand (Fountas and Pinnell 2017b).

Knowing how to provide scaffolding by introducing a new book to a group of students is incredibly useful when supporting a book club with a new, challenging text, and I would argue that book introductions, similar to those we use in guided reading, are just as essential when students set out to read longer, more complex chapter books.

A well-planned book introduction serves a few purposes. First, it piques readers' interest in the book. You've probably had the experience of talking to a friend who raves about a book they've just finished, describing it in such a way that you immediately order it or check it out of the library. At the end of a great book introduction, students should be chomping at the bit, eager to get their hands on the new book.

Second, a book introduction serves as scaffolding—support to stretch students beyond their independent ability. As students move into longer, more demanding texts, they will face new challenges as readers, such as multiple conflicts, more characters who exhibit increased complexity, more literary language, and gradual and nuanced character development, just to name a few. Just because a student can decode these texts doesn't mean they are accessing all the complexities buried within them. Book introductions can provide students access to deep levels of comprehension they might not control completely on their own.

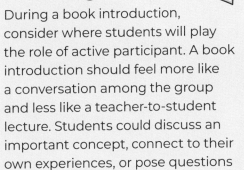

**Teaching TIP**

During a book introduction, consider where students will play the role of active participant. A book introduction should feel more like a conversation among the group and less like a teacher-to-student lecture. Students could discuss an important concept, connect to their own experiences, or pose questions they're curious about.

Third, a great book introduction sets readers up for some new complex thinking by planting the seeds before they've even read. In other words, it can provide a lens that helps them see even more in a text. While students may not be noticing and thinking about how Astrid's jealousy impacts all her relationships in *Roller Girl*, if we bring students' attention to that fact, they are more likely to recognize it and think about it. This also means they are more likely to bring their ideas about it to the book club discussion.

As you work with your clubs, leave room to be flexible with your introductions. A group new to a text level band or new to a genre would probably benefit from a heavier book introduction, while another group might be able to read the blurb on the back and get on with it. In one fourth-grade classroom, I met with a book club to give them a book in the I Survived series. They were on their third book in the series and were very familiar with the structure, the author, and ways to mine for deeper themes and messages. They grabbed the book out of my hand, read the blurb and first chapter themselves, and were off.

That same day, however, I gave the introduction below to a book club whose members were taking on a more challenging text than they were used to *and* were new to the genre of fantasy. I wanted to set them up for both the text and genre.

**Book Club:**
Recess Queens

**Title of Book:**
*The Secrets of Droon*

**Teacher:** This is one of my favorite series, so if you like it, I can find you more. It's similar to that book we read, *The Secrets of Droon*. It's similar in that these three kids get transported, not to a different world, like in *Secrets of Droon*, but to a different time. These three kids are time travelers. Isn't that interesting? They get transported to a different time. Can we just flip to the back? We're going to read the blurb together. "How did Joe, Fred, and Sam end up in King Arthur's court?" King Arthur is a famous king during medieval times.

**Solei:** Do they go back? Do they come back?

**Teacher:** Remember how in *Secrets of Droon* they were trying to come back to their normal world? Are you trying to figure out if they come back?

**Solei:** (nods)

**Teacher:** That's their quest! To try to figure out how to come back! "It all started with *The Book*, a present from Joe's magician uncle. One minute they were looking at pictures of knights in *The Book*—and the next minute they *are* knights, battling fire-breathing dragons and gross-smelling giants! Can the Time Warp Trio escape death and destruction—and make it back to the twentieth century in time for lunch?"

**Teacher:** So I want to show you a couple of things. In Chapter 1, they're right in medieval times. They're already battling a knight. In Chapter 2, it flashes back to when they were in the kitchen, and it tells you about *The Book*. Does that make sense?

**Katrina:** So like it starts in the middle and then it goes back to the beginning.

**Teacher:** That's right. That's a little confusing—just know that it has a flashback. I want to show you some funny things. In Chapters 1 and 3, they're fighting a knight. The knight keeps using funny language. Can you turn to page 3? Can you look at the picture of this knight? What are you noticing about him?

**Shayla:** Because of this (pointing to a feather on the knight's helmet).

**Katrina:** Really big.

**Solei:** I thought that was his leg.

**Katrina:** A tornado (pointing to the lance).

**Teacher:** It's used by knights to stab. It's called a lance. He also has a sword. Do you know what—

**Solei:** A suit?

**Teacher:** That's right. A suit of armor. He also talks funny because it's from medieval times. Can you find on page 3 where it says, "None shall pass"? Can you say that?

**All:** None shall pass!

**Teacher:** ". . . boomed the Black Knight."

**Shayla:** What does "boomed" mean?

**Teacher:** Can you ask your group that question?

**Katrina:** Maybe trying to say we're going to win you! When it says "boom"!

**Teacher:** It says he says it in a super loud voice to show he's going to beat them. The knight always talks in a funny way. Sometimes you'll have to figure out what he means. And sometimes the boys will tell you. So in this part, can you guess what he means by "none shall pass"?

**Solei:** No one shall pass.

**Katrina:** No one can ever, like, pass him?

**Teacher:** That's right! He says it funny but you figured out what he means.

**Solei:** Does he speak another language?

**Teacher:** Kind of. He speaks a different kind of English. Here he says, "Thy tongue and garb art passing strange. Methinks thy band hails not from this shore." Fred says, "What did he say?" And another boy says, "He said we look funny and we're probably not from around here." Do you see how he talks funny?

**Solei:** How does he know what he said?

**Teacher:** I know! He figured it out just like you figured it out for "None shall pass!" So sometimes you'll do the work of figuring out what the knight said. One last thing, the knight calls them a bunch of weird things. He calls them wizards. He calls them sorcerers. Do you know what a sorcerer is? It's like a wizard. He also calls them enchanters. Do you know what an enchanter is?

**Katrina:** Like a wizard?

**Teacher:** Like a wizard! He calls them these words because—

**Katrina:** Enchanter is kind of a magic kind of word.

**Teacher:** We're going to read Chapters 1 through 4. They're going to be battling knights almost the whole time. When we come back together, we'll talk about how they overcame all these challenges they're facing. Sound okay?

As with any teaching method, we make decisions about the degree of support students might need. I say "might" because it's usually an educated guess. Sometimes I plan for heavy support and realize students could have done much of the work on their own. Sometimes I think they just need a quick summary and realize that I should have provided more explanation about the changing narrators. Each group, each day, each book will require varying degrees of support from you.

If you are supporting younger readers, or readers new to book clubs, or readers who are trying a new text level or genre, you may need to provide a heavy introduction. Here are a few considerations to keep in mind as you plan to introduce a new text to a book club.

First, consider the deeper meanings embedded in the text. Traditionally, a book introduction includes a summary of major plot points, but my hunch is that most readers are already reading with that lens in mind: "What's happening? What are the big events here?" In a heavy introduction, encourage readers to ask deeper questions, like "What are some things this book is *really* about? What are the deeper meanings?" In a book introduction for *Front Desk*, you might say, "In this book, Mia and her parents have just arrived in California from China. The parents have found work at a motel, and Mia has offered to help at the front desk. As an immigrant herself, Mia becomes very aware of how different immigrants experience this country. She watches and notices how people are mistreated at school, by the police, and by other immigrants looking to get a leg up. As a result, Mia feels compelled to help other people who are experiencing similar hardships." With this brief statement, we're setting the book club up to read beyond merely tracking Mia's jobs and interpersonal conflicts. Our hope is that students start right in searching for deeper themes about immigrants, the promise of America, compassion, and solidarity.

Another thing that might pose new challenges for readers tackling texts at new levels is the complexity of the text structure. In early chapter books, the reader tends to follow the main character, who tells the story from their perspective. In more sophisticated chapter books, the narrator might change, along with the perspective of the story. For example, in *Wonder*, chapters switch from Auggie's perspective to that of his friends. In even more complex texts, readers might not find out until later in the book how the different characters' stories are connected.

Another challenge readers might need support with is the order in which certain parts of the book are presented. When students are new to the I Survived series, they'll benefit from knowing that Chapter 1 starts in the midst of a historical disaster, followed by a flashback that slowly leads up to the time of Chapter 1. The last chapter then flashes ahead to give the reader a vision of how the main character was impacted. Without a brief introduction to this timeline, readers might become confused and lose interest.

It's also worth considering what language or words could potentially get in the way for readers. There's no way to introduce every word readers will have trouble with, nor should we try. This is especially true when book clubs are reading chapter books. However, you might show an example of a sentence, a phrase, or a word that will support them throughout the text. You could highlight any of the following elements:

- Use of dialect or accents in realistic or historical fiction (e.g., medieval language in *Time Warp Trio* Book 1)

- Use of invented languages in fantasy (e.g., "muggles" and "disapparate" in Harry Potter)

- Unfamiliar or content-specific words in nonfiction or realistic fiction (e.g., "levees" and "ward" in *I Survived Hurricane Katrina*)

Since we use shorter books in primary grades, a book introduction is just a fraction of the small-group lesson. After the introduction, the students might stay with the teacher, who listens to individual readers to prompt and reinforce strategic actions. With longer texts in book clubs, however, that introduction might be the lesson in and of itself. If a student is reading a 250-page book, it does little good to lean in and listen to them read the first two pages. Instead, you might introduce the book and then send them off to read independently before they meet, a day or two later, for their book club discussion.

While this level of support might be necessary for some book clubs in some cases, keep in mind that the goal is independence. Toward this goal, you might also teach book clubs about ways that adults set themselves up for success rather than relying on someone else. You could teach them how to read a blurb on the back of the book, read the first few pages, and talk about what they already know and what they want to figure out. A book club might even read a published review to get a sense of the book's deeper messages. A book introduction is just one of many ways you can support a book club toward independence. Across the year, keep an eye on the ways you're teaching clubs—not just about the books they are reading but about the behaviors, skills, and processes that will help them work in authentic ways with less and less support.

## During Reading: Running Alongside the Reader

A friend of mine was planning to run her first marathon and decided to hire a running coach. Rather than standing on the sidelines of a track, the coach went on a long run with her, watched her form, and eventually noticed that she wasn't lifting her legs up high enough as she got fatigued. The coach continued to run alongside her, prompting her to "lift your knees" and "lengthen your stride." Over and over my friend heard this prompt and soon found that whenever she went running, even on her own, the voice of the coach was ringing in her ears. Even without the coach there, she was able to notice her knees and her stride and prompt herself to correct her form.

As reading teachers, we can borrow some techniques from this running coach. First, the coach did not stop the runner over and over again to explain or coach. She ran next to her, prompting her to focus on one thing. When we run alongside readers, we don't want to interrupt them too often or for too long, since this also interrupts their process of making meaning and following the story or the information.

The coach didn't talk too much as she ran alongside. Instead, she focused her attention on a single thing (knees/stride) and kept her prompts short and consistent ("knees up" and "lengthen your stride"). We've all had experiences when we realize we are overexplaining, repeating ourselves, or rephrasing our point so many times our students' eyes glaze over. But we have to remember to keep it brief, to the point, and consistent so that our students are clear on the strategy we are teaching.

The other strength of the running coach is her ability to focus on one thing and let the other things go. I'm sure there were other areas of improvement my friend needed as a novice marathon runner, but her coach kept the focus on her knees and length of stride. Changing the focus and coaching for too many things can overwhelm learners, both cognitively and emotionally. As we run alongside readers, we might make note of other strategies that would be helpful, but we stay clear about the one area we've chosen to focus on so as not to overload our readers.

Coaching book clubs "on the run" can be challenging even for experienced teachers. To prepare myself for this challenge, I like to follow a predictable structure when designing comprehension-focused lessons for book clubs. Figure 5.2 lays out the four instructional steps I anticipate needing to take as I "run alongside" my students. It also provides my rationale for taking each step, as well as examples of the language I plan to use. Following this table, I discuss the four steps in detail.

| PART OF LESSON | TEACHER LANGUAGE | RATIONALE |
|---|---|---|
| **Establish** | "I've noticed that you . . . (compliment)" <br><br> "So today I'm going to teach you . . ." | Recognizes strength-focused approximations and provides rationale for the instruction, connecting the point to how it helps the club members as readers. |
| **Teach** | "Watch me as I . . ." <br> and/or <br> "Let's try this together." | Provides groups with a vision for this new work or a scaffolded opportunity for practice. |
| **Coach** | "Now it's your turn to try this as your read." <br><br> (Coach individuals as students read.) | Provides readers time to independently practice the strategy with the assistance of a teacher. |
| **Rename** | "As you continue to read, remember to . . ." | Reminds students of the new work they should continue to do in the future and how it relates to a larger goal. |

### Establish

Any time I work with a book club, I want it to feel like a special invitation into the "literacy club" rather than a punishment for a deficit, and this informs the way I set the stage with the first few sentences. What messages am I sending students if I begin my lesson with something like this: "I noticed your book club isn't analyzing characters from multiple angles. You're just naming simple character traits and moving on." Even if this is said in the kindest tone, the implicit message is that they're doing something wrong and I'm out to fix them, or worse, punish them. On the other hand, I might lean in and say something like this: "Last time I listened to your book club talk, I noticed you were doing some really sophisticated work as you thought about the characters. You were really trying to figure out who they are as people, what's motivating them, why they're acting the way they are. Well, since you're already working on that, I think I could show you something that would help you understand those characters even more. Do you want to try?" The implicit message here is this: "You're doing good work. I think you're ready for something that will help elevate what you're already doing." That's an invitation few students turn down. For the book club reading *Fox*, I might say, "I noticed that you're really trying to figure out Fox's motivation, or *why* he's doing what he's doing. In the kinds of books you're reading now, characters are getting more complex. So I think you're ready to analyze the many parts or motivations of the characters."

## Teach

Once you've introduced the group to the new work, it's time to do some teaching. Just naming the strategy you want them to learn will rarely be enough support for students to take on new work. Effective teaching also involves showing and coaching. So for the next part of the lesson, decide *how* you'll teach this strategy.

One option is to demonstrate, using your own thinking and a familiar book. You might use a novel students have heard during read-aloud or have read previously as a club and think aloud in front of them. As this group learns to unpack characterization at deeper levels, I might say, "Can you watch me do this work in *The Poet X*? I've been thinking about how Xiomara is so brave and fearless in her notebook and how she has the strength to say really hard things to her brother when she needs to. On the other hand, she acts really different with her mom. Whenever she's around her mom, she's like a fortress. She doesn't really talk or share or express herself in any way. It's like she doesn't trust her mom and so she can't really be herself. This makes me think she's cautious about who she reveals herself with." With this think-aloud, I'm demonstrating how readers go beyond static character traits to analyze how characters have multiple layers and how they're affected by their relationships. Providing proficient models is an essential part of teaching anything new, so a powerful demonstration can lift the level of students' thinking, showing them a possible next step.

Another way into this is through shared practice. If you're returning to a book club on another day for more instruction around the same strategy *and* you're confident you've already provided a clear demonstration, you might provide an opportunity for some shared practice. For example, instead of showing students my thinking, I could say, "Can we think together about how sometimes characters show different sides of themselves depending on who they're with? Let's think and talk together about the character of Baby Mouse, from our class read-aloud. In some scenes, she's by herself. What kind of person is she when she's on her own in her room? What about when she's with her best friend, Wilson? What other sides does she show? What do you notice about her when she's with Felicia Furrypaws? How does she change?" In this way, students have the opportunity to practice the strategy together while you coach them into deeper and more complex thinking.

## Coach

While you have the ability to provide heavier and lighter scaffolding during this teaching, you don't want to spend too much time modeling or facilitating shared practice. After all, the power of any small group lesson is that it provides time to coach students while they try the work in their own book. Keep the "teaching" section of the lesson brief—just a few minutes—so that the majority of the time is spent with students reading their own books while you coach them. Immediately after you teach, whether through modeling or through shared practice, ask students to read their books and try out the strategy you've taught.

Independent practice and coaching are the real meat and potatoes of the lesson. It's when students read and you "run alongside" each reader for a bit, briefly asking about their thinking, and prompting them to try the new strategy. Colleen Cruz, a staff developer at The Reading and Writing Project, used to say that during this part of the lesson we should coach like a basketball coach from the sidelines—but far less aggressively. The coach doesn't stop the game, she doesn't give a speech about practice last week, she doesn't deliver paragraphs of information. More likely, she uses short, brief phrases to remind players to employ a technique she taught them earlier. "Pressure the ball," she might say to the defense. "Seek the contact!" she might remind the forward. Similarly, teachers should avoid interrupting readers with too much teacher talk. With this in mind, wait a minute until the students are all reading independently. Then lean over to a student and ask them to "turn up your voice" slightly so you can listen to them read for a minute or two. When you hear an opportunity, you might ask, "What parts of the character are you seeing here?" After the student talks for a bit, you might say, "Keep reading. See if you notice other sides of the character." Then, move to another student in the group and repeat.

Moving from student to student in this way, coaching individuals, provides an opportunity for the highest level of differentiation. If a student immediately shows evidence of taking on the strategy, you can name that for them. You could say, "You're noticing how complex the characters are in this book—that they aren't just one way all the time." On the other hand, if a student needs more support, you can step back into demonstration or shared practice right in the moment. Ideally, this shared practice would take place within the student's text. However, if you haven't read the text yet (which happens sometimes), it's helpful to have a familiar book on hand so that you can practice on a shared text together.

## Teaching TIP

Plan teaching, prompting, and reinforcing language for each small group beforehand so that you can quickly and concisely switch back and forth, all the while sticking to your teaching point.

Some days, you'll have time to individually coach every student in the book club as they read. Other days, you'll need to prioritize students who need more support. Though this time is flexible, I tend to give myself about ten minutes for coaching.

One final caution before we move on. As you plan, teach, and coach, keep in mind that there are hidden dangers when we teach skills in isolation. The danger for teachers is that we lose sight of the long game—finding enjoyment and meaning making in texts. We might teach for mastery of a skill or strategy and then monitor only whether students are employing that skill or strategy, not whether it's helping them uncover the deeper meanings of text. The danger for students is that they become so metacognitive, so focused on thinking about their thinking, that doing so distracts them from the meaning of the book. As I mentioned earlier, the idea of making a personal connection to a character isn't the end goal; it's a means to an end. Readers relate to characters so that they can better understand them, walk in their shoes, and emotionally connect to the story or topic. This is all to say that, as we coach readers, it's worth remembering that we need to monitor whether they are trying a new strategy and—at the same time—whether doing so is helping them understand the book, develop their own ideas and, ultimately, become stronger readers.

### Rename

You can end each lesson the way you began, by naming explicitly and clearly for students what you taught them and what you'd like them to practice. It's helpful to use the exact same words you used in the beginning of the lesson for the sake of clarity. Of course, each day's teaching isn't an isolated event. It fits within the context of your unit of study, so students have also learned something from your focus lessons and from your reflection time at the end of the workshop. We don't expect that they will practice one thing at a time, because that's not what proficient readers do. Instead, you're inviting students to add the new focus strategy to the repertoire of strategies they're learning—in other words, to add it to their toolbox. After renaming the strategy you just taught, you might add, "Remember, this is just one more way to develop and revise more complex ideas about the characters in your book, to understand them as you understand real people in your lives."

In the transcript below, I teach students by briefly modeling the strategy in the class read-aloud, then coaching individuals in their book club book, *Flora & Ulysses*.

| ESTABLISH | **Teacher:** You know, I was listening to your club talk the other day and I was noticing that some decisions the author made were really bugging you. That happens to me as a reader often. Like, "Why did the author make the character do that?! Or say that?!" When you notice a decision the author makes that bothers you, it's worth stopping and really thinking about why the author did that, because often the author is trying to teach us something. |
|---|---|
| | What I want to teach you today is that those are places worth talking about. That's why I gave you some sticky notes. So you could actually jot a little thought and stick it on the page, and that way you're ready to talk about it. |
| TEACH | **Teacher:** I just wanted to show you an example, and then you're going to get started reading. I was just reading this little part about Meg [in *A Wrinkle in Time*], and I keep noticing that she's whining and whining and whining. She feels very whiny to me, and that bothers me. And I did that thing where I asked myself, "Why did the author do that? Why did she make Meg whine so much?" And I was thinking maybe the author is trying to teach me, you know, how Meg is the least evolved character and the least wise. Maybe the author is trying to teach me that when you're not so wise, you whine a lot, and the wiser you are, the less you complain. |
| | Maybe. |
| | So you see how I just jotted myself a note, and now I'm ready to talk to you about it? So as you read, you've got some sticky notes, you can stick them on your page to remind yourself. Remember to ask, whether you like something or you don't, "Why did the author do that? What might they be teaching me?" So get started reading wherever you are. Go ahead. |

**Teacher:** Elizabeth, what are you thinking? What are you noticing here?

**Elizabeth:** Her mom's not even paying attention. Like looking down. Just typing, typing.

**Teacher:** That's interesting. So say more about that.

**Elizabeth:** Like Flora is trying to see if her mom is paying attention. She said, "I could stop breathing." And her mom was basically like, "I'm busy." And her mom never says she's beautiful and doesn't say she loves her.

**Teacher:** So then it's worth asking, "Why is the author making the mom act like that?" What are you thinking about that?

**Elizabeth:** Well, she's always too busy . . . for Flora.

**Teacher:** So what do you think Kate DiCamillo is trying to say there?

**Elizabeth:** That even though she's a mom, she doesn't take care of Flora like . . . like moms do? Sometimes parents don't take care of the kids, and kids have to take care of themselves.

**Teacher:** Hmm, so parents don't always do their jobs well. Keep reading and see if there are other parts that fit with that idea.

**Teacher:** What are you thinking so far, Bryan? Are you noticing anything?

**Bryan:** No. I had a question. Why would she talk to the squirrel, but the squirrel can't understand?

**Teacher:** What are you thinking about that?

**Bryan:** Probably because she's bored?

**Teacher:** What do you think about that idea—that Flora is bored?

**Bryan:** I don't know.

**Teacher:** You're not sure.

**Bryan:** No.

**Teacher:** So let's read a little bit, and let's see if there are any parts the author did something you either like or don't like about a character. And then we'll try to ask why. Go ahead and read out loud to me a little bit.

**Bryan (reading aloud):** *"Flora Belle!" her mother shouted. "I can hear you up there talking to yourself. You shouldn't talk to yourself. People will hear you and think that you're strange."*

*"I'm not talking to myself!" Flora shouted.*

*"Well, then, with whom are you speaking?"*

*"A squirrel!"*

*There was a long silence from down below.*

*And then her mother shouted, "That's not funny, Flora Belle. Get down here right now!"*

**Teacher:** What are you noticing there? What are some of the decisions Kate DiCamillo is making about the character? About both characters?

| | |
|---|---|
| | **Bryan:** The mom didn't even notice the squirrel! She thinks she's kidding! |
| | **Teacher:** The mother didn't even notice! So let's take that and ask that question again. What might Kate DiCamillo be trying to teach us by having her talk to her squirrel, knowing that her mother barely notices her? What do you think Kate DiCamillo is trying to teach us? |
| | **Bryan:** If you don't pay attention to kids, they have to find other friends. Maybe she's talking to the squirrel so much because she's lonely? |
| | **Teacher:** Interesting. So that might be a place where you stick a Post-it, because you have an idea about Kate DiCamillo, what she's trying to teach us there. I wonder, too, Bryan, if there are other parts where she gets lonely and has to find other friends. If you could, keep track of that as you continue to read. Keep going. |
| **RENAME** | **Teacher:** Can you all come to a stopping place? As you continue to read this book, and when you start the next book with your club, can you keep asking yourself that question, "Why did the author write that?" You might ask it when some part really rubs you the wrong way, or you might even ask it when you like a part. Either way, the author is making a decision, and it's important to ask why they made that decision. |

As soon as students start developing ideas about the topics and characters they're reading about, you've got a clear sign they're ready for some teaching about talk—how to put an idea forward, how to respond to each other's ideas, and how to grow and develop new thinking through the conversation. Even the simplest idea can be made more nuanced and complex through an engaging discussion with other readers who have been thinking about the same text.

## Teaching for Conversation in Book Clubs

Pulling a chair up next to a book club or inviting students to have their book club discussion at my table allows me to do a few very important things. First, as I discuss in Chapter 4: Utilizing Talk as an Assessment, it allows me to listen closely and collect some data about what students are doing in terms of comprehension (what they're thinking about the text) and conversation (how they're talking to each other about their thinking). It also gives me a chance to teach them something new and coach them as they try it on. To teach conversation skills during a book club discussion, you have a few options. Your approach will depend upon how much scaffolding and support the book club needs and your preference for planning or responding in the moment.

## Explicit Teaching to Launch the Conversation

When readers are just beginning to learn how to have effective book club conversations, you can tap into the same structure I outlined earlier to help them focus on comprehension while they're reading—establish, teach, coach, and rename. However, for this option, rather than teaching a comprehension skill, you'll be working on a conversation skill, perhaps providing some sentence frames and demonstrating either by yourself or with a proficient partner. You then launch the conversation and coach individuals to try out the new skill while they are in the midst of the conversation. Prompting students while they're having a conversation can be distracting, so Serravallo (2010) suggests "whispering in" prompts or sentence starters that support students to "think or talk in a new direction" (147). Finally, you can end the lesson by renaming your teaching point and providing an example of how the students have tried out this new work.

For instance, in my assessment of the book club reading *Separate Is Never Equal* in the previous chapter, a next step for the club is to begin to paraphrase each other's ideas so that people feel heard and so that they are tracking the bigger ideas being discussed. For this club, I provide a few sentence frames, like the ones in Figure 5.3, to help members paraphrase and to model how they might listen to a club member talk and then paraphrase their idea to make sure they understood (**establish** and **teach**).

Then, I quickly invite the group to begin their discussion and try this new strategy. While they talk, I listen for an opportunity for one of them to paraphrase another's idea. If I hear an opportunity and they don't take it, I move into a coaching role. While I could pose a question, such as "Who can paraphrase what Liliana just said?" I find that it's quicker and more supportive to suggest some specific language. I quickly say, "So you're saying . . . ," and give the students a minute to try this language on for themselves. Paraphrasing each other over and over is needless and distracting. However, during a conversation, I might listen for a couple of appropriate times when students could apply the new strategy in a purposeful way (**coach**).

I like to end this type of lesson by naming for the group how they used, or approximated, the strategy I just taught. I say, "Did you notice how Liliana was talking about how the parents are fighting for justice, and Miguel paraphrased to make sure he was understanding her? Paraphrasing can also help the person speaking. Sometimes you aren't sure exactly what you mean, and a paraphrase can help clarify it in your own mind. Sometimes it just feels good because it lets you know your club is really listening closely to what you have to say" (**rename**).

For this type of lesson, you can plan ahead by charting sentence frames and deciding how you'll use this language in a demonstration. You can also plan the prompts you'll use once students start their discussion.

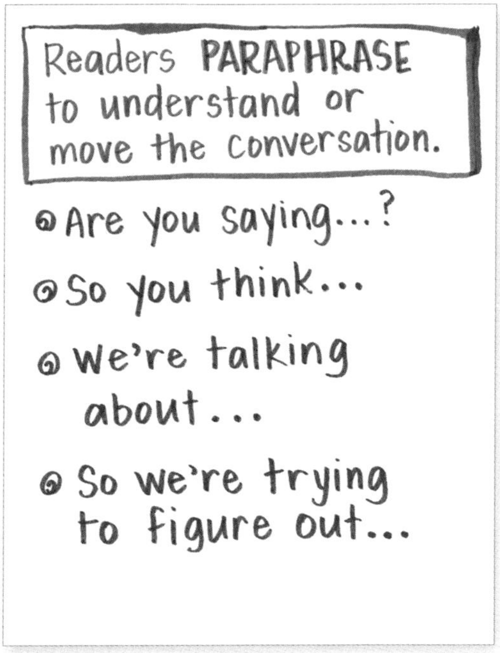

> Readers **PARAPHRASE** to understand or move the conversation.
> - Are you saying...?
> - So you think...
> - We're talking about...
> - So we're trying to figure out...

Figure 5.3

## Giving a "Time Out"

Sometimes I watch my son's soccer team scrimmage at the end of practice. Often, the coach will blow the whistle and ask the kids to freeze right where they are. She'll remind the kids of a play or a drill they just practiced and show them (very briefly) how they can use that play during an actual game. Then, she resets their positions and asks them to "play on" using what she just taught. It's an incredibly effective way to transfer an isolated skill or play they learned in a drill *into* the actual play of the game.

We can use this same methodology with book clubs. Just as the coach watched the kids scrimmage, you can first spend a bit of time listening to the book club conversation and decide in the moment what you need to teach. Once you make a decision, you can ask the students to "take a time out" from the conversation. You won't want to stop the conversation for too long, because they might lose their flow. Just like the coach, name something you noticed, teach them something, or remind them of something you've already taught, and then say, "Give it a go!" Just like in soccer, you're teaching them to use an isolated skill and then placing it in the context of a meaningful conversation.

This option works best if you're comfortable teaching by responding in the moment. Just remember, teaching is not the same as reminding or prompting. If you see a need and you haven't explicitly named it and demonstrated it, it's probably best to save it for another time and address it with an explicit teaching point. A "time out" is usually a quick reminder of something you've already taught.

## Reinforcing by Noticing and Naming

Another teaching move we can borrow from the soccer coach is noticing and naming an effective strategy. During the first quarter of the game, a player on my son's team panicked every time the ball came near him. He punted it up the field toward the goal. He did this without thinking about who he was kicking it to, and more often than not, the other team stole the ball. During the second quarter, however, each time the ball came to him, he kept it close, dribbling down the field while he scanned for a teammate to pass to. This led to many more successful passes and two shots at the goal. During halftime, his coach pulled him aside and said, "I noticed how you controlled the ball that time. When you dribbled and passed to your teammate, you were able to keep the ball in our control and make more shots on the goal." The coach named what the player was doing and the effect it had on the team. By naming, with generative language, a strategy a student uses, we can increase the chances they'll use it again.

This approach tends to work best in the middle or at the end of a book club conversation. After listening and observing closely, you can ask the group to stop their conversation for a moment. Describe what you just observed and tell them how it helped their understanding or conversation. Many times, students use strategies without an awareness of their use. They may be using them successfully but unconsciously and inconsistently. By naming what they did, when they did it, how they did it, and why it was useful, we can help make the use more conscious and deliberate. In *Choice Words*, Peter Johnston calls this noticing and naming the "central part of apprenticeship" (2004, 12) and suggests that awareness and the ability to notice are closely related to power and the learner's sense of agency. The best part about this approach is how students often puff up (or blush) with pride as a teacher raves about them. And of course, noticing and naming a strength helps kids develop positive identities as readers and as club members.

## Three Methods for Teaching Conversation During Talk

| METHOD | PURPOSE | EXAMPLE |
|---|---|---|
| **Explicit Teaching** | ■ to introduce a new strategy<br>■ to provide a clear model and vision for new work<br>■ to provide a heavy scaffold | Today I want to teach you something new. When someone shares their idea about a character or a topic, it's worth thinking, "What do I think about that?" and pushing yourself to respond. You might respond and add on by saying things like this:<br>"Yes, and . . ."<br>"Also . . ."<br>"That makes me think . . ." |
| **"Time Out"** | ■ to transfer something taught in isolation to an authentic context<br>■ to help students use a strategy on the run | Last week we learned about responding to each other's ideas before moving on to a new one. You might agree, disagree, give some specific examples, or just elaborate on that idea. Let's try again, and instead of moving on, let's respond to Johana's idea about the character. Johana, can you say your idea again? |
| **Reinforcing** | ■ to foster a sense of agency<br>■ to help students develop positive identities as readers and as club members<br>■ to bring awareness to an effective strategy | I noticed that when Johana stated her idea about the main character, rather than moving on to a new idea, Justin responded and added on. This helped the group stay on a single topic and develop a sophisticated idea about the main character. Responding and building on to each other helps build complex ideas. Can you keep doing that? |

The good news (and maybe the bad news?) of teaching is that you've got lots of choices to support the decisions you need to make. Planning your instruction for comprehension and conversation in book clubs is about selecting the method that best matches the goal you've set for each group. If I want to introduce a book club to a new author in a challenging new genre, I'll make sure I provide a heavy book introduction before members begin to read. If my goal for another club is to get readers past character analysis and into more interpretive readings, I'm going to need to model and coach them as they read. If another club has individuals with deep ideas, but two members just wait for their turn to share rather than contributing to a conversation, I may choose to provide a "time out" during their talk and coach them to respond to each other's ideas. Planning, teaching, and responding to clubs takes a wide repertoire of tools in our teaching tool belt and the flexibility to strategically and intentionally use them all.

# CHAPTER 6

# Growth over Time

R ECENTLY, I HAD a conversation with a veteran teacher who was reflecting on a major shift in her teaching. "I used to plan two weeks at a time based on the demands of the curriculum. But the more that I listen to students as they read, and assess the ways they talk to each other, the more I find myself planning short term. Sometimes I plan only a few days at a time. And now I'm planning such different things for each book club."

She went on to share how she'd previously used the curriculum and standards as the sole driver for her teaching. Since the curriculum was already written, she could plan ten to fifteen days at a time because, in her mind, her responsibility was to the curriculum. To me, this is an excellent and necessary place to start. It's also a necessary practice to outgrow. Once we know more about our students, what they are approximating, what they are controlling, and what they still need to learn, our responsibility shifts from exclusively teaching curriculum to additionally considering the needs of our students.

As this teacher closely observed the book clubs in her classroom, she also recognized a need to differentiate instruction for each club, because she noticed their different needs around skills and strategies. Where in the past she might have met with book clubs to reteach or reinforce her whole-group lesson, she now saw book clubs as an opportunity to plan targeted instruction that built on the strengths and needs of each group.

If you think of it from the students' perspective, this is really living the dream—interacting with a teacher who observes you closely to see what you *can* do and what you're *attempting* to do, learning new skills and strategies that are tailored to your needs, and receiving support for each new skill until you can control it independently. Isn't that what we all want for ourselves as learners and for our own kids?

In all honesty, this kind of teaching is challenging. It requires a few essential characteristics in a teacher. First, it requires a belief that our job is to take students into account when we plan our instruction. Curriculum can be a very useful guide, but by not looking closely at how students are reacting—intellectually and emotionally—to the curriculum, we miss opportunities for greater impact.

This kind of teaching also requires flexibility. We can carry carefully prepared plans and intentions into our work with book clubs and still respond to them flexibly. In order to do this, we establish and eventually remove the necessary scaffolding students need to take on new work and gradually transfer that to independent practice.

Flexibility is even more essential when we remember that we will get it wrong now and then. Sometimes, I come to a book club with a highly planned demonstration and realize halfway through that students are already doing what I planned on teaching them. I have to switch right in the moment or sheepishly say, "We'll try again tomorrow." Other times, I plan on some light support through coaching but realize in the middle of the conversation, "They don't understand what I'm asking them to do! They need a clear model!" I have to quickly plan a brief demonstration or come back with a different plan the next day.

When I first began teaching book clubs, whether I was introducing a new book, teaching while groups were reading, or teaching in the midst of a discussion, it took me ages to plan each lesson. I struggled to find the perfect bit of text to demonstrate, I wrote and revised the precise words I would use to coach, and I made adorable charts with my best handwriting. While I still consider planning and preparation to be essential, each year I become more efficient and more comfortable flexibly teaching "on the run." On-the-run teaching is different from "winging it." "Winging it" implies that nobody really knows where we're going or what we're doing. Teaching on the run is responsive. It requires an internalized repertoire of teaching techniques and strategies that you can pull from at any given moment to purposefully and clearly respond to a club with deliberate instruction.

Teaching responsively also necessitates holding two competing ideas in our head at the same time. We are simultaneously looking for immediate, small shifts and long-term growth. Both students and teachers need quick wins. This can only happen if we are consistently collecting data (by listening to students' conversations) and using it for our immediate teaching. The short game informs our teaching tomorrow or the next day. The short game helps us ask the questions "What did students take on from that lesson? Who needs more support next time?" During these short cycles of assessment-driven instruction, I'm looking for approximations and noticing inconsistent progress. Expecting mastery isn't realistic for short cycles because mastery and deep understanding are long-game goals. And after years of guiding book clubs, I readily admit that a short-game mindset can be a double-edged sword, because early progress is not always linear. Skills students seem to have one day may be shaky the next. Comprehension strategies mastered in fiction don't automatically transfer when we shift into reading poetry. Because of this, looking *only* at the short game can be frustrating and disheartening—and unfair to students.

## Looking for Shifts over Time

In his book *Mentor Author, Mentor Texts* (2011), Ralph Fletcher compares teaching to planting saplings. He recalls the day he spent with an eighty-year-old man who was planting baby trees, knowing full well that he would never see them in their complete splendor or get to enjoy their shade. This, Fletcher says, is like teaching—you plant the seeds even though you might never see the full growth.

Teaching students to read texts deeply, to think, react and respond, and to share this process with others, thus growing beyond their individual abilities—all this is no quick work. It takes more than individual teachers; it takes entire systems of support to ensure that, year after year, students are provided rich texts, opportunities to talk and be listened to, and immediate feedback that helps them grow.

Teachers who are new to book clubs might think, "My kids aren't ready for this. They don't know how to talk to each other." Returning to Fletcher's metaphor, we would never imagine saying, "This sapling isn't ready to grow." Instead, we would ask, "What does it need to grow and thrive?"

Every classroom teacher knows the feeling of wondering, "Is my teaching even having an impact? Are kids learning what I'm teaching?" When we are in the head-down, day-to-day grind of a classroom, it's challenging to see the ways in which students are growing. But the long game is planting the saplings. The long game is believing that deep understanding, mastery, and the ability to generalize and transfer take years and years. The long game is noticing how a student who never spoke in September begins asking questions of their book club in May, or how a student who once dominated the conversation now invites a quieter peer into the conversation by saying, "Jefferson, it looks like you have something to say." The long game means that we periodically step back and look at shifts not from one day to the next but from one quarter to the next or one season to the next. It's important for us to acknowledge that while growth and change may be challenging to see between Tuesday and Thursday, they're often glaring in the best way if we compare January and May.

This spring, I spent four months working with a book club in fourth grade. Across those four months, I alternated between listening to assess their book club conversation, teaching them how to develop ideas about the texts they were reading, and teaching them how to sustain a conversation by building on each other's ideas. As the summer break drew closer, I had one of those "Is this even making an impact?" moments and thought it might be helpful if I looked back at the students' growth across the semester. Let's take a look at three transcripts I took of one book club between February and May. In the first transcript, we'll observe this group during their second time ever meeting together.

At their first meeting, the students selected a novel and decided to read the first three chapters. I wanted to stay out of the way as much as possible during this second meeting to get an initial idea of their independent ability to understand the text (comprehension) and discuss the text (conversation).

| | |
|---|---|
| **Book Club:** The Torpedoes<br>**Meeting Date:** February 12 (second meeting)<br>**Title of Book:** *Friend or Fiction* | |

**Teacher:** Who would like to get us started? Carlos?

**Carlos:** Yes.

*(45-second pause)*

**Teacher:** What were some of the things you were noticing and thinking about in Chapter 3?

*(45-second pause)*

**Teacher:** Carlos, did you have something you wanted to say about the book?

**Carlos:** No, that's okay.

**Teacher:** Okay, who can get us started?

**Roshni:** Can I?

**Teacher:** Go ahead.

**Roshni:** In the beginning, in Chapter 1 and 2, I feel that she's kind of lonely . . . because when she was in the cafeteria, she's kind of sitting there alone because her friend was late so she sat there alone and watched everyone planning stuff with their friends and eating with their friends.

*(60-second pause)*

**Teacher:** Does it feel like you're not sure what to say next?

**Carlos:** No.

**Teacher:** Okay, could you try to respond to Roshni?

**Carlos:** What?

**Teacher:** Could you try to say something back to Roshni?

**Angel:** What did she say?

**Teacher:** Roshni is going to say her idea again and any of you three can respond to her, say something back to her.

**Roshni:** I feel she's a bit lonely because her friend was late and everyone else was planning things with their friends or eating with their friends so she kind of felt lonely.

**Steven:** Like Roshni said, maybe she's lonely because her friend was coming late and other children were playing with their friends. That might give us ideas about what the book might be about.

**Teacher:** Carlos, can you respond to Roshni now? She said her idea again.

**Carlos:** I'm not sure what I'm supposed to say.

It is immediately clear that this group wasn't even sure what a book club was supposed to do together. Students seemed to be waiting for me to make the first move or pose a question. Most of the students weren't sure how to begin the conversation, despite several invitations to do so. What's also clear from this transcript is that students didn't seem to be aware of their responsibility to listen and respond to each other. When Carlos realizes he was supposed to be listening to Roshni, he asks me, rather than her, what she's just said. Steven has a sense that he's supposed to say something, so he repeats back Roshni's idea almost verbatim. One of the students, Victoria, doesn't say anything.

In my experience, this type of passive and disconnected interaction is not uncommon when book clubs first meet. Even students who have had experience participating in book clubs before can be stilted and awkward as they establish a new dynamic and identity together. At the same time, if my ultimate goal is to teach students to function with agency and independence, I need to be very deliberate about my teaching, providing some heavy scaffolding in the beginning and then strategically lightening those scaffolds as students begin to orchestrate the conversation on their own.

In this next transcript, taken two weeks later, we'll see some small shifts as students become more comfortable with each other and begin to take a more active role.

**Book Club:** The Torpedoes
**Meeting Date:** February 24 (fourth meeting)
**Title of Book:** *Friend or Fiction*

**Teacher:** Would anyone like to get us started today?

**Carlos:** On page 100, what was her name? The made-up character's name?

**Roshni:** Zoey?

**Carlos:** Yeah. Jade and Clue got into an argument. Clue had feelings for her and they got into a big argument.

**Teacher:** What did that make you think about, Carlos?

**Carlos:** That Clue was hiding the secret for a long time.

**Teacher:** What did that make you think about the Clue and Jade?

*(pause for 45 seconds)*

**Steven:** I just read Chapter 9 when Clue gave her the book back. She's been patient enough. Clue was talking weird stuff that she didn't understand. He said he brought Zoey to real life. She was confused by that and surprised.

*(pause)*

**Roshni:** I have one note about how she learned about friendships. Friends won't always be there. But now I'm seeing that Zoey changed it for Jade—friends WILL be there when you need them.

**Steven:** And when I was reading, Jade thought about what Mrs. Yang told her—that writers can make things possible.

**Teacher:** How does that fit with what Roshni just said?

**Steven:** Because writers can be friends, other writers can help you make it happen.

Just two weeks later, I can see some shifts starting to happen. We had been working hard on not only summarizing an important part but sharing our thoughts, reactions, and ideas about that part. I see that I was doing some heavy coaching of Carlos ("What did that make you think?") and that Steven and Roshni were able to share their ideas. And though I had to prompt Steven to connect his comment to Roshni ("How does that fit with what Roshni just said?"), he was able to explain the connection easily. Students were showing that they could share an idea and add on, with support and prompting from me. The most important shift I saw was that they were listening to each other! I didn't need to prompt them to listen, or respond, or ask them to repeat themselves. I also noticed that Victoria was still not participating in the conversation. I learned right after this meeting that she was having trouble monitoring the plot of the story and so it was challenging for her to participate in these discussions about character relationships and lessons and themes.

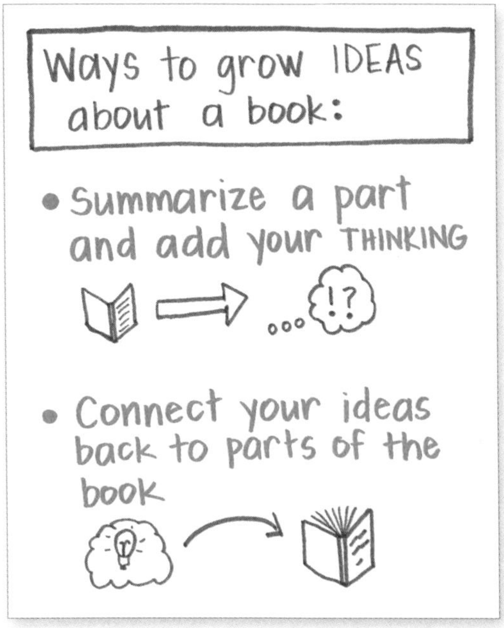

Figure 6.1

Over the course of the next few weeks, I taught the group ways to move beyond literal understanding and expand on their ideas. The strategies I taught (see Figure 6.1) were useful not only during the book club discussion but also while the students read independently and while they jotted about their thinking to prepare for the discussion. These teaching points grew directly out of needs I observed during the book club conversations.

In this next transcript, taken three months after the book club first started meeting, notice the tremendous shifts this group was able to make.

---

**Book Club:** The Torpedoes

**Meeting Date:** May 12

**Title of Book:** *Diving With Sharks! And More True Stories of Extreme Adventure!*

---

**Steven:** I learned something on page . . . when it was talking about coral running out of air, that section? I learned that they were talking about dangers for the animals, and dangers for them. She wouldn't have time to help the coral if she ran out of air. Also land stuff affects ocean or sea stuff. So that taught me that everything we do here, on the earth, can also— The fish in the water can also feel it.

**Carlos:** There's a place where divers cannot go . . . like sixty-five meters.

**Steven:** And when the person was running out of air, she only had fifteen minutes. And in those ten minutes, she couldn't find her other partner. Because she needed two partners to get out of the water. But she was panicking but then she told herself, "Try to stop panicking," because then big trouble can happen.

................................................................

(30-second pause)

................................................................

**Teacher:** So there are two ideas on the table. One is about how what we do on earth connects and affects the ocean. The other idea is about . . .

**Carlos:** Like garbage! Garbage pollutes the water, then we cannot drink it anymore. Then we would die!

**Roshni:** I agree. Plastic is one of the things that pollute the water too.

**Steven:** I agree too. Like oil. When people used to bring the ships with oil. Some of the oil fell into the ocean and that made different animals and fishes die because of that.

**Roshni:** And because of that, a lot of animals are dying.

**Carlos:** Like turtles versus straws. Turtles swallow straws, then they die.

**Teacher:** How does that connect to the book?

**Steven:** All of those researchers, all they want to do is learn more about the animals. They also want to see the dangers that it causes them that we might do. It also shows us facts about the animals.

**Carlos:** They might be researching about what is killing the animals.

**Steven:** I agree, because maybe they want to research about the animal because they don't want people to kill them. Those animals are like us, they eat, they look for homes, they want to survive! We survive the same way—we eat, we have our own house. But we also try to kill them.

**Victoria:** I'm thinking that it's not bad to kill animals sometimes but sometimes it's bad because some people get the newborns that haven't gone out by themselves because their parents have gotten them and they were soon gonna get older but then people kill them and then they don't get to grow up.

**Roshni:** I agree, because sometimes you have to kill the animals to eat, but if you're just doing it for . . . let's say "fun," I don't know why, but maybe *that's* bad. But maybe hunting isn't as bad.

Looking at this transcript from three months later, what stands out most is how little I'm doing as a teacher. The students now demonstrate an understanding that they should bring ideas about the book to launch a discussion without me even asking. Steven is eager to start by putting two separate ideas on the table. One move I make in the beginning is to paraphrase the ideas up for discussion ("So there are two ideas . . .") in an effort to highlight the importance of building on a single idea for a while—but I don't even get my whole paraphrase out before Carlos responds and the conversation is off and running again.

Over the few weeks prior, I had been doing some heavy work with the group around ways to keep their conversation going (see Figure 6.2 on the following page). You can see evidence of this when Roshni agrees and adds on and Carlos provides examples that connect. They're truly listening to each other and responding, rather than adding unrelated thoughts.

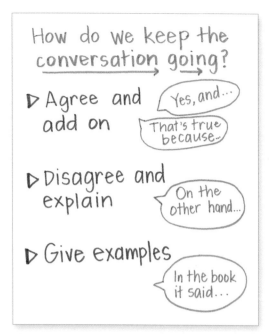

How do we keep the conversation going?

▷ Agree and add on
- Yes, and...
- That's true because...

▷ Disagree and explain
- On the other hand...

▷ Give examples
- In the book it said...

**Figure 6.2**

The conversation picks up momentum, but as I notice the discussion straying away from the book, I prompt the students to connect their powerful ideas back to what they've read ("How does that connect to the book?"). Steven makes a deep connection that scientists study animals to understand the threats to their existence. And with this, a new line of thinking develops. Victoria, who speaks the least, looks across the table at me like she has something to say. She is often silent unless I directly invite her to contribute, but now, for the first time, she adds a new line of thinking ("I'm thinking that it's not bad to kill animals sometimes") without my involvement.

What I loved most about this conversation was how I couldn't get a word in, nor did I *need* to. While the day-to-day shifts were incremental, the progress across these three months was enormous. At the end of the conversation, I asked the group, "How did that feel?" Steven looked at the group. "That was great," he said, his pride evident. I shared parts of the transcript with them, highlighting where they added on, supported their thinking with examples, and connected the idea back to the book.

## Following Rules Versus Making Decisions

As I've established, I'm a terrible cook. Or more accurately, I hate cooking so I just never got good at it. (Or maybe I never got good at it so I hate it?) Yet somehow, I've amassed a shelf full of cookbooks. I've received them as wedding presents and birthday presents, and even bought some for myself when the pictures were particularly enticing. Once in a while, I look for a recipe, gather the ingredients, follow each step meticulously, and place a little sticky note at the top edge of the page to remind myself I am capable of this tiny victory.

And then one day, I heard the chef Samin Nosrat talk about her new cookbook, *Salt Fat Acid Heat* (2017). Surprisingly, there aren't many recipes in this cookbook. Instead, Nosrat spends the bulk of the book describing the four elements of cooking she says that all cooks, from professional chefs to Jewish grandmothers, consider in order to cook delicious food. In the introduction, Nosrat writes that her cookbook is designed to help "guide you as you choose which ingredients to use, how to cook them, and why last-minute adjustments will ensure that food tastes exactly as it should" (5). Nosrat wrote a book that fosters the freedom to be flexible while cooking, to make a tentative plan and revise based on the ingredients in front of you, and to take calculated risks that lead to new experiences.

*Better Book Clubs* is designed with the same principles in mind but for book clubs. You'll find some ideas to get you started in the appendices that follow, but there is no curriculum or set of lessons that could possibly tell you everything you need to know to create and foster successful book clubs and engaged readers. What works for you might be too structured or rigid for a teacher across the hall. What led to student success one year might lead to apathy the next. I wish there were a recipe for success, but kids are humans, and our classrooms are tiny, complicated worlds. This complexity is also the beauty and power of student-centered teaching.

Once you have the tools, it's up to you to innovate beyond what I suggest here. When it comes to responsive, student-centered teaching, there are no rules to be followed, only decisions to be made.

# Appendices

## Appendix A: **Noticed/Next Steps Matrix**

| | CONVERSATION | COMPREHENSION |
|---|---|---|
| **Noticed** | | |
| **Next Steps** | | |

**Book Club Planning Document**

| Book Club Members: |
|---|
| |

| Goal: |
|---|
| |

| Teaching Point: |
|---|
| |

| Teaching Language | Coaching Language | Reinforcing Language |
|---|---|---|
| Demonstration text, page number: | | |

| Names | Notes/Observations |
|---|---|
| | |
| | |
| | |
| | |

# Appendix C:

# Touchstone Anchor Charts and Sample Lessons

In this appendix, you'll find resources to support you and your students as you launch, develop, and extend book clubs. Over the years, I've found that I regularly encounter some common challenges, which the teaching points in the following pages address. While this is not an exhaustive or comprehensive collection, these lessons meet many of the needs that arise in book clubs.

The lessons listed in the following table correspond to the six anchor charts included in this appendix. The charts develop in sophistication from Beginning to Developing to Advanced and are typical of charts I share to support clubs as they progress along a continuum toward greater student independence.

| STAGE | FOCUS AREA | GOAL | PAGE |
|---|---|---|---|
| **Beginning** | Comprehension | Jotting Thoughts to Prepare for Discussions | 114 |
| | Conversation | Working Well in Book Clubs | 116 |
| **Developing** | Comprehension | Developing Thoughts Across the Book | 118 |
| | Conversation | Growing Ideas Through Discussion | 120 |
| **Advanced** | Comprehension | Exploring Deeper Themes and Ideas | 122 |
| | Conversation | Listening and Supporting Thinking | 124 |

Each anchor chart establishes a goal at the top, written in student-friendly language. Under each goal are a handful of strategies that help students work toward the goal. Each strategy serves as the focus of a single lesson. For instance, since the anchor chart on page 118 has three bulleted strategies, you could build it across three individual lessons, each centered on a bullet point. Of course, your students' strengths and needs will help you make decisions about the pace of the lessons, which ones to extend, and which ones to compress.

I suggest building each anchor chart as you go, adding only what you've taught so far. I used to make beautiful charts ahead of my lessons and then laminate them so that I could use them year after year. But I noticed that a premade chart prevented me from being responsive, because I relied on the chart, rather than on the students in front of me, to determine what I taught next.

Next to each anchor chart, you'll find a sample lesson for the first bullet point, along with some suggested teacher language. Each lesson features a slightly modified version of the structure for teaching book clubs discussed in Chapter 6 (Establish, Teach, Coach and Reinforce, Rename). I tend to lean more heavily into this structure when I'm introducing a new teaching point, then lighten the scaffold in future lessons by coaching and reinforcing more, rather than modeling. As you observe students taking on each new strategy, you can repeat the sample lesson structure to teach the remaining strategies bulleted on the anchor chart.

You'll likely find it most effective to teach these lessons to your entire class during the minilesson portion of your workshop. You can then differentiate your support for each book club as needed. Some book clubs might need the lesson to be retaught with another demonstration. Other clubs might just need some in-the-moment coaching to take on a new strategy. And still others might try a new strategy immediately and move right along with some basic reinforcing from you. The length of time you spend on each teaching point will vary by the needs of each book club. For instance, you might teach a lesson once to one book club, while another book club will need to work on it for a week or more.

While these anchor charts, teaching points, and sample lessons are touchstones I return to year after year, I find that I'm always revising them, adding additional scaffolds (like the sentence stems), or trying new language. Consider them a starting place. Curriculum and resources are most powerful when put in the hands of an observant and responsive teacher, so adopt or adapt the following pages as needed to support your learners best.

# Readers jot their thoughts to get ready for their book club discussion.

- A question you have

- An idea or thought you have (about the topic or characters)

- What you're confused about

- A part you loved (or hated) and why

# SAMPLE LESSON

| | |
|---|---|
| **Establish** | **Teacher:** Readers, it's been exciting watching you start to work with your book clubs. Now that you're meeting regularly, one of the things I've noticed is that sometimes your book club is kind of quiet for a few minutes in the beginning because you are all trying to figure out what to talk about or how to start the conversation. So I thought today I might teach you something important about book clubs. You don't want to wait until you meet with your book club to think about what to talk about. That's something that you can do as you read. Readers jot their thoughts as they're reading as a way to prepare for their book club discussion. Today, I'm going to teach you one way to do this. |
| **Teach** | **Teacher: One way to jot about your thinking is to write down a question you're wondering.** If you're reading a story, you might ask a question about the characters, why they're doing what they're doing, and what's going on underneath the surface. If you're reading a nonfiction book, you might learn some new information, and that will lead to some new questions. Watch me try this as I reread a little bit from [insert familiar text here, such as the class read-aloud].<br><br>[Read an excerpt aloud]<br><br>　　So the book just said . . .<br>　　Now I'm wondering why . . .<br>　　I'm also wondering how . . .<br><br>You'll notice that questions that start with "why" or "how" might lead to big discussions because there's often no one right answer. Those are the kinds of questions that are perfect for book clubs to discuss.<br><br>As you read today, I'm going to coach you to stop and jot some of the questions you have. |
| **Coach and Reinforce** | **Teacher Coaching:** What's going on here? What are you wondering? You can jot that down.<br><br>**Teacher Reinforcing:** You stopped at a part where you had a question and now you can jot it down. |
| **Rename** | **Teacher:** Remember that as you're reading, you can jot questions you have about the topic or characters to prepare for your book club discussion. I bet you'll figure out other ways to jot about your thinking too. |

NOTE: As you observe students taking on this new strategy, you can repeat this lesson structure to teach the remaining strategies bulleted on the anchor chart.

BEGINNING

Conversation

Working Well in Book Clubs

# Book clubs work well together.

- Make a reading plan and commit to it!

- Bring materials to the book club so we're ready to talk.

- Find our club house quickly and get started as soon as possible.

- Leave time to reflect on our conversation and our club goals.

# SAMPLE LESSON

| | |
|---|---|
| **Establish** | **Teacher:** Readers, do you ever meet with your book club and find that the first few minutes feel kind of awkward because there's no plan and you're not sure what to do first? Or you start the conversation and then run out of things to say before the time is up? Today, I thought I could teach you something that might help your book club run more smoothly. Some book clubs like to make a plan, also known as an agenda, so that meetings are predictable and go more smoothly. |
| **Teach** | **Teacher: Today, I'm going to help you make a plan with your book club.** I'll share a few things that book clubs do together, then as a club you'll need to select which ones you want to try. You'll make an agenda for your time together.<br><br>Here are a few things book clubs do together: [Chart out suggestions.]<br><br>▪ Look through their ideas and pick a few worth discussing<br>▪ Discuss an idea<br>▪ Reflect on how the discussion went<br>▪ Set a talk goal for the next discussion<br>▪ Set a thinking goal for future reading<br>▪ [Add additional things clubs can do that come to mind.]<br><br>Which items do you want to put on your book club agenda? Talk with your book club for a few minutes and jot down a plan, or an agenda, that you'll try. |
| **Coach and Reinforce** | **Teacher Coaching:** What things do you want to do together? What order makes sense for your club?<br>**Teacher Reinforcing:**<br>So, you decided to . . .<br>That plan will help your book club . . . |
| **Rename** | **Teacher:** This week you'll have a chance to try the items on your book club agenda. You can always change it if it's not working. In a few days, you'll check in with your book club to see if the plan you made is working or if you'd like to revise it. |

NOTE: As you observe students taking on this new strategy, you can repeat this lesson structure to teach the remaining strategies bulleted on the anchor chart.

BEGINNING

Conversation

Working Well in Book Clubs

**DEVELOPING**

**Comprehension**

**Developing Thoughts Across the Book**

# Readers develop thoughts and carry them across the book.

- Notice an important detail or part and ask yourself, "What does that make me think or wonder?" Try to answer your question.

- Test out your idea with other parts of the book.
  - Does this part fit with your idea?
  - Do you need to revise your idea?
  - Do you have a totally new idea?

- Look across your ideas and ask, "How do these ideas fit together? What is my theory <u>now</u>?"

# SAMPLE LESSON

| Establish | **Teacher:** I've noticed that sometimes during read-aloud, there seem to be parts that just make us stop or gasp or yell out. We know something important is happening in that part and we have these strong reactions. I'm thinking about when I was reading *Big Red Lollipop* and Katherine yelled out, "WHY?" at the part when the girl calls Sally and she's worried Sally thinks she's weird. Remember how Katherine said, "WHY?" |
|---|---|
| | Something important was happening there. So today I want to teach you something new. **When you're reading and you notice an important detail or part, it's worth asking yourself, "What does that make me think or wonder?"** And then you might do some thinking and try to answer your question. |
| **Teach** | **Teacher:** I want you to watch me try this with the part from *The Big Red Lollipop*. |
| | Katherine (and a few of you) were asking why. I'm going to do a little thinking there. |
| | Maybe it's because . . . |
| | Or maybe it's because . . . |
| | I wonder . . . |
| | So now I'm thinking . . . |
| | [Think aloud using the stems above. Model how you can try to answer your own question and develop an idea.]. |
| **Coach and Reinforce** | **Teacher Coaching:** What feels important about that part? What are you wondering? What are you thinking? |
| | **Teacher Reinforcing:** |
| | You noticed . . . |
| | So you pushed yourself to have a thought . . . |
| | You pushed yourself to ask a question . . . |
| **Rename** | **Teacher:** As you read today, if you have a strong reaction or notice an important part, don't just keep reading. See if you can push yourself to have a thought or ask a question. You might even try to answer your question or bring it to your book club. |

NOTE: As you observe students taking on this new strategy, you can repeat this lesson structure to teach the remaining strategies bulleted on the anchor chart.

# Book clubs grow ideas through their discussions.

- Summarize a part and then share a reaction or a thought.

  > In this part . . . That makes me think . . .

- Connect your ideas back to the book.

  > For example . . . The part that makes me think that is . . .

- Test out an idea by supporting it with multiple parts of the book.

  > The parts that fit with my idea are . . . For example . . .

- Explore an idea from different perspectives or angles.

  > One the one hand . . . But on the other hand . . .

# SAMPLE LESSON

| | |
|---|---|
| **Establish** | **Teacher:** Club, I've been listening to you talk, and one thing I'm noticing is that one of your strengths as a club is figuring out which are the really important parts of the book. Yesterday you spent some time retelling a few scenes that seemed particularly important to the character's journey. And because you're doing this, I thought I could teach you something new that will help you start to grow your ideas. Are you ready? |
| **Teach** | **Teacher: One thing book clubs do together is grow ideas. And one way to do that is to summarize an important part. THEN, you'll want to push each other to have a reaction or a thought about that part.** That reaction or thought can lead to some pretty great discussion, since everyone in the club might have a different reaction or thought. So you might summarize and then say, "This made me feel . . ." or "This made me think . . ."<br><br>Or if someone else summarizes, you might ask them, "How did you feel about that part?" or "What did that part make you think?"<br><br>Watch me try this with the book we just read as a class, *Drawn Together*. This part really stood out to me, where the dragon comes up out of the chasm. I'll summarize, and then can one of you ask me what I thought or felt about that part?<br><br>In this part, they thought they had found a connection, but the feeling of distance comes back to them. (Pause)<br><br>**Student:** What did that make you think or feel?<br><br>**Teacher:** Well . . . I was sad at first because I thought they were done with feeling distant. But now I think that drawing didn't solve everything forever. They're still going to have to work hard to feel close. But I'm also thinking they have the tools now, because the picture shows the grandson with the grandfather's tool. And the grandfather has the grandson's tool. So I think it's complicated between them now.<br><br>Did you see how you helped me grow an idea by asking me what the part made me feel or think?<br><br>As you talk today, listen for someone to summarize a part and see if you can help them grow an idea. |
| **Coach and Reinforce** | **Teacher or Student Coaching:** What did you think or feel about that part?<br><br>**Teacher Reinforcing:** You heard her summarize a part, so you asked her to add on her thinking! That helped the group grow her idea. |
| **Rename** | **Teacher:** Remember that when you're together, you can help each other grow an idea. One way to do that is to summarize a part and then add on your feeling or thinking about that part. |

NOTE: As you observe students taking on this new strategy, you can repeat this lesson structure to teach the remaining strategies bulleted on the anchor chart.

# Readers explore deeper themes and ideas from the text.

- Notice repeating objects, images, or lines of text. Ask yourself, "What might this represent or mean? Why might this be important?"

- Analyze the character's behavior, decisions, and dialogue. Ask yourself, "What's <u>really</u> going on here? What might this <u>really</u> be about?"

- Name a *big* theme or topic from the *book*. Ask yourself, "What might the author be saying about that theme or topic?"

# SAMPLE LESSON

| Establish | **Teacher:** Readers, you've been noticing that in many of the books you're reading—graphic novels, picture books, and chapter books—there's often an object or a line of text or even an image that keeps repeating. And when you notice that it's repeating, that means the author is trying to tell us something. The author isn't going to tell us directly what it means. **It's our job as readers to ask, "What might this mean or represent?"** |
|---|---|
| Teach | **Teacher:** I want to show you how one of your classmates, Joseline, did this. She noticed a repeating object in one of our read-aloud books, *Tough Boris*. She noticed that the violin keeps appearing over and over. And at the end, the boy is playing for the pirate. She asked herself, "What might this mean? What might the violin represent?" She thought it might represent a small act of kindness. Her idea was that by showing a little kindness, the boy really changed how the pirate acted. The violin kind of softened him. So the violin might represent kindness and the effect it has on others. |
| | She might not have come up with that idea if she had just ignored the violin. But she noticed this important object and she stopped and asked, "What might it mean or represent?" |
| | As you read today, be on the lookout for objects, lines, or images that seem important. |
| Coach and Reinforce | **Teacher or Student Coaching:** What are you noticing? What objects/lines/images have you noticed might be important? What might that mean? What might that represent? |
| | **Teacher Reinforcing:** You noticed . . . |
| | You asked yourself, "What might that represent or mean?" |
| Rename | **Teacher:** As you continue to read, keep an eye out for repeating objects or lines or images. When you see something, stop and ask yourself, "What might this mean or represent?" |

NOTE: As you observe students taking on this new strategy, you can repeat this lesson structure to teach the remaining strategies bulleted on the anchor chart.

# Book club members listen and support each other's thinking.

- Ask club members to elaborate on their ideas.

  > Say more about . . . Can you elaborate on . . . ?

- Invite quieter voices into the conversation.

  > Do you have something to say? Can we hear what _____ has to say?

- Paraphrase someone's thinking to make sure you understand them.

  > So you think . . . Are you saying . . . ?

- Summarize the big ideas of the entire book club discussion.

  > Now that we've talked, we're thinking . . . On the one hand, we're saying . . . On the other, . . .

# SAMPLE LESSON

| Establish | **Teacher:** I've been listening in on your conversations recently and I've noticed a strength of your club: You're reading in such a way that you have a lot of strong ideas that you're putting forward. When someone puts an idea forward, rather than moving on or adding on, it's your job as a club to explore that idea. **One way to explore an idea is to ask the person to say more about it or elaborate on it.** You might say something like this:<br><br>"Can you say more about that?"<br><br>"What do you mean?"<br><br>"Can you give us some examples of that?" |
|---|---|
| Teach | **Teacher:** I'm going to say my idea about something, and I'd like for one of you to push me to explore or elaborate. My idea is . . .<br><br>**Students:** Can you say more about that? |
| Coach and Reinforce | **Teacher or Student Coaching:** Can you say more about that? What do you mean by that? Can you give us some examples?<br><br>**Teacher Reinforcing:** You pushed him to say more. You asked for examples, and that helped him elaborate. |
| Rename | **Teacher:** As you continue your discussions, look for opportunities to coach each other to elaborate on your ideas. That will help you explore and develop those ideas. |

NOTE: As you observe students taking on this new strategy, you can repeat this lesson structure to teach the remaining strategies bulleted on the anchor chart.

# Bibliographies

## Professional Bibliography

Allington, R., and R. E. Gabriel. 2012. "Every Child, Every Day."
    *Educational Leadership* 69(6): 10–15.

Barnhouse, Dorothy, and Vicki Vinton. 2012. *What Readers Really
    Do: Teaching the Process of Meaning Making.* Portsmouth, NH:
    Heinemann.

Burkins, Jan, and Kari Yates. 2021. *Shifting the Balance: 6 Ways to
    Bring the Science of Reading into the Balanced Literacy Classroom.*
    Portsmouth, NH: Stenhouse.

Calkins, Lucy. 2015. *Reading Units of Study: Learning Progressions.*
    Portsmouth, NH: Heinemann.

Clay, Marie. 2016. *Literacy Lessons Designed for Individuals.* 2nd ed.
    Portsmouth, NH: Heinemann.

Fletcher, Ralph. 2011. *Mentor Author, Mentor Texts: Short Texts, Craft
    Notes, and Practical Classroom Uses.* Portsmouth, NH: Heinemann.

Fountas, Irene C., and Gay Su Pinnell. 2017a. *The Fountas & Pinnell
    Literacy Continuum: A Tool for Assessing, Planning, and Teaching.*
    Portsmouth, NH: Heinemann.

———. 2017b. *Guided Reading: Responsive Teaching Across the Grades.*
    2nd ed. Portsmouth, NH: Heinemann.

Glover, Matt, and Mary Alice Berry. 2012. *Projecting Possibilities for Writers: The How, What, and Why of Designing Units of Study, K–5*. Portsmouth, NH: Heinemann.

Guthrie, J. T., and Nicole M. Humenick. 2004 "Motivating Students to Read: Evidence for Classroom Practices that Increase Reading Motivation and Achievement." In *The Voice of Evidence in Reading Research*, Peggy McCardle and Vinita Chabra, eds. Baltimore: Paul H. Brookes Publishing Co.

Johnston, Peter H. 2004. *Choice Words: How Our Language Affects Children's Learning*. Portland, ME: Stenhouse.

Lamott, Anne. 1994. *Bird by Bird: Some Instructions on Writing and Life*. New York: Anchor Books.

Lindfors, Judith Wells. 1999. *Children's Inquiry: Using Language to Make Sense of the World*. New York: Teachers College Press.

Nosrat, Samin. 2017. *Salt, Fat, Acid, Heat: Mastering the Elements of Good Cooking*. Illustrated by Wendy MacNaughton. New York: Simon and Schuster.

Parten, M. B. 1933. Social play among preschool children. *The Journal of Abnormal and Social Psychology* 28(2): 136–147.

Pearson, P. D., and M. C. Gallagher. 1983. The instruction of reading comprehension. *Contemporary Educational Psychology* 8(3): 317–344.

Ray, Katie Wood. 2006. *Study Driven: A Framework for Planning Units of Study in the Writing Workshop*. Portsmouth, NH: Heinemann.

Serravallo, Jennifer. 2010. *Teaching Reading in Small Groups: Differentiated Instruction for Building Strategic, Independent Readers*. Portsmouth, NH: Heinemann.

Zwiers, Jeff, and Marie Crawford. 2011. *Academic Conversations: Classroom Talk That Fosters Critical Thinking and Content Understandings*. Portland, ME: Stenhouse.

## Children's Literature Bibliography

Abbott, Tony. 1999. *The Secrets of Droon: The Hidden Stairs and the Magic Carpet.* Illustrated by Tim Jessell. New York: Scholastic.

Acevedo, Elizabeth. 2020. *The Poet X.* New York: HarperTeen.

Blabey, Aaron. 2016. *The Bad Guys.* New York: Scholastic.

Brown, Peter. 2011. *You Will Be My Friend!* New York: Little, Brown Books for Young Readers.

Cooper, Abby. 2019. *Friend or Fiction.* Watertown, MA: Charlesbridge.

DiCamillo, Kate. 2015. *Because of Winn-Dixie.* Somerville, MA: Candlewick.

———. 2016. *Flora & Ulysses.* Somerville, MA: Candlewick.

Fox, Mem. 1998. *Tough Boris.* Illustrated by Kathryn Brown. Boston: HMH Books for Young Readers.

Gurevich, Margaret. 2016. *Diving with Sharks! And More True Stories of Extreme Adventures!* Washington, DC: National Geographic Kids.

Henkes, Kevin. (1996). *Sheila Rae, the Brave.* New York: Greenwillow Books.

Holm, Jennifer, and Matthew Holm. 2005. *Babymouse #1: Queen of the World!* New York: Random House.

Jamieson, Victoria. 2015. *Roller Girl.* New York: Dial Books for Young Readers.

Khan, Rukhsana. 2010. *Big Red Lollipop.* Illustrated by Sophie Blackall. New York: Viking.

Lê, Minh. 2018. *Drawn Together.* Illustrated by Dan Santat. Los Angeles: Disney Hyperion.

L'Engle, Madeleine. 2007. *A Wrinkle in Time.* New York: Square Fish.

Lowry, Lois. (1989). *Number the Stars*. Boston: Houghton Mifflin Harcourt.

Palacio, R. J. 2012. *Wonder*. New York: Alfred A. Knopf.

Reynolds, Jason. (2017). *Long Way Down*. New York: Atheneum/Caitlyn Dlouhy Books.

Rowling, J. K. 1998. *Harry Potter and the Sorcerer's Stone*. Illustrated by Mary Grandpre. New York: Scholastic.

Scieszka, Jon. 1998. *Time Warp Trio, No. 1: Knights of the Kitchen Table*. Illustrated by Lane Smith. New York: Puffin Books.

Steinkellner, Emma. 2019. *The Okay Witch*. New York: Aladdin.

Tonatiuh, Duncan. 2014. *Separate Is Never Equal: Sylvia Mendez and Her Family's Fight for Desegregation*. New York: Abrams Books for Young Readers.

Wild, Margaret. 2006. *Fox*. Illustrated by Ron Brooks. Sydney, Australia: Allen and Unwin.

Yang, Kelly. 2019. *Front Desk*. New York: Scholastic.

# Index

*f* = figure, *t* = table

growing ideas through, 120
ideas worthy of, 57
jotting to prepare for, 105, 112, 114–115
in read-aloud book clubs, 32–33
shifting to, from retelling, 11–12
summarizing points, 55
teaching conversation skills during, 91–93
discussion topics, 25–27, 26f
*Diving with Sharks! And More True Stories of Extreme Adventure!,* 104–106
Duff, Stacey, 43

elaborating and clarifying, 54, 124–125
establish
agendas, 117
deeper themes and ideas, 123
developing thoughts, 119
growing ideas through discussion, 121
jotting as concept, 115
listening and supporting thinking, 125
as step in teaching during reading, 85–86, 85f, 92, 113
examples
language in new text, 83
methods for teaching conversation, 95
supporting ideas with, 54, 57–58, 61–62, 64–65, 74

fishbowl conversation, 14, 15, 31
Fisher, Suzanne, 32
flashbacks, 79, 82
Fletcher, Ralph, 99, 100
flexibility
with club-managed schedule, 44
differentiated teaching, 98
in group formation, 36–41
in lesson planning, 70
*Flora & Ulysses,* 89–91
Fountas, Irene, 67
*Fox,* 26–27, 55–57, 59–60, 74, 86
*Friend or Fiction,* 101–103
*Front Desk,* 82

genre, introducing, 77–81
Glover, Matt, 73
goals
anchor chart, 112
crafting, 73–75
evaluating, 75
examples and non-examples of, 74f
long-term, 18–19
versus strategies, 73
grade-specific book clubs. *See* sixth grade book club; third-grade book club
gradual release of responsibility model, 19
graphic novels, 39
grouping options, 37–41
growth. *See also* student independence
demonstrated through transcripts, 100–106
from long-term to short-term planning, 97–99
looking for shifts over time, 99–106
recognizing, 100
*Guided Reading,* 67
guidelines, whole-class conversation, 24–25

Harry Potter, 49–50, 83
*Houndsley and Catina,* 37

ideas
building on and challenging, 54–55, 61, 64
building toward complex, 33
discussion-worthy, 57
growing through discussion, 120–121
meaning-making and, 59–60
paraphrasing, 92
putting on the table, 57, 58, 61, 62, 74, 75
sharing versus building on, 30
shifting from retelling to discussing, 12–13
student-suggested, 26–27
supporting with examples, 54, 57, 58, 61, 62, 64, 65
teacher's, 26f
and themes, deeper, 122–123
ways to grow, 104f